The Musings Of An Urban Monk

Simon Jones

First published in Great Britain in 2014

Instant Apostle
The Barn
1 Watford House Lane
Watford
Herts
WD17 1BJ

British Library Cataloguing-in-Publication Data

A catalogue record for this book is available from the British Library

This book and all other Instant Apostle books are available from Instant Apostle:

Website: www.instantapostle.com

E-mail: info@instantapostle.com

ISBN 978-1-909728-18-9

Printed in Great Britain

Instant Apostle is a new way of getting ideas flowing, between followers of Jesus, and between those who would like to know more about His Kingdom.

It's not just about books and it's not about a one-way information flow. It's about building a community where ideas are exchanged. Ideas will be expressed at an appropriate length. Some will take the form of books. But in many cases ideas can be expressed more briefly than in a book. Short books, or pamphlets, will be an important part of what we provide. As with pamphlets of old, these are likely to be opinionated, and produced quickly so that the community can discuss them.

Well-known authors are welcome, but we also welcome new writers. We are looking for prophetic voices, authentic and original ideas, produced at any length; quick and relevant, insightful and opinionated. And as the name implies, these will be released very quickly, either as Kindle books or printed texts or both.

Join the community. Get reading, get writing and get discussing!

Acknowledgements and comments

These Writings have been written over two and a half years as a series of reflections each month. With the encouragement of a few friends, it started to seem like the Lord was prompting us to publish them. To my amazement, they seemed to flow in the order they had been written. They are a two-and-a-half-year journey, so it's worth saying that my understanding of some of the depths of silence written about early on as 'silence is golden' had had another two years of experience by the time I wrote about similar things in the final four reflections.

There have been two main influences on my spiritual journey which are worth mentioning.

The first has been different ministries, teachings and books which have focused on the Father's love. Amongst these have been Father's House Trust, Fatherheart Ministries, Father's House Europe, and Father's House Bala. Thanks to Steve and Katy Cardell, Robert and Vicki De Hoxar, James Jordan and Jeff Scaldwell. James and Jeff will most likely have no idea how significant my few brief meetings with them and their ministries/teachings have been in my life.

The second has been different aspects of contemplative spirituality, retreat centres I have visited, and one or two really key people who have encouraged me down this path. Thanks to Keith and Linda Entwistle, Sue Perks, the occasional monk or nun I have run into, and many different leaders of all kinds of Christian retreat centres. I've been blessed to be able to visit about 20 in the past ten years.

Thank you to all for the encouragement!

Thank you Nathalie, beloved one, for sharing the beautiful journey!

Thank you Abba for accepting me as I am!

Just a short word on the title. When Steve suggested it to me, I couldn't resist! It's a fab title! To me the word 'monk' signifies a calling to a life of prayer. That has certainly characterised the last ten years of my journey. I even have the word in my email address! However, I have no wish to wear the word or the title as a label. I have taken no life vows; I have no rule of life. To me my truest identity is Simon, the beloved of God. My identity is hidden in God at a depth beyond my ability to understand, and certainly beyond any labels man could put on me. Also the word 'urban' applies for now, but who knows for the future – I love the countryside! That all said, it's a great title.

Contents

Foreword

This is what the Lord *says: 'Stand at the crossroads and look;
ask for the ancient paths, ask where the good way is, and walk
in it, and you will find rest for your souls.'*
Jeremiah 6:16

Rest for your souls – that is something we all seek, isn't it?
Whether we are someone who relishes adventure and living life
passionately at 100mph, or someone who prefers a quieter time
– at the end of the day, I don't think there are many amongst us
who don't also hope it will bring rest for the soul. That sense of
satisfaction, a day well lived, all is well, I'm happy, I'm at
peace. Sadly, these are actually quite elusive feelings for many
of us in this full and demanding, expectations-high age,
dominated by drive and performance.

But there is a promise tucked into this verse in Jeremiah, a
promise that indicates that rest for our souls is out there, that
we can find it. But first we have to stop – to stand at the
crossroads and look, to ask for the ancient paths, to ask where
the good way is, and then to walk in it. And for me, that is at
the heart of retreating, at the heart of the vision behind the
Urban Retreat. Sometimes it is good, indeed necessary, to stop
for a while, to reflect, to be refreshed, to be reminded of what
really counts and to regain perspective, that we might go on to
walk again. And when we walk again, we have found the way
to walk, or better yet, the One with Whom we walk – and that
can bring rest to our souls in a way that nothing else can.

There is a hunger, an ache even, for time out in our society.
God drew my attention to this when He first put the dream of
an Urban Retreat on my heart – I was not the first person to
notice it and I will not be the last. The need is deep and
pervasive, well documented in fact – life is fast and can be
furious, and most of us know that we can't keep going on like

that indefinitely. Yet, even in our knowing it, many of us also struggle with the stopping of it – we need help to do it! As a result I was prompted to pursue an Urban Retreat – a place on the doorstep, not a two-hour drive away, that might make accessing the space and peace a little more doable.

As a child, I used to love secret places – hidden dens under big bushes or behind the bed, where I could be tucked away from the world. When God started speaking to me about the Retreat, He showed me that He had put that desire on my heart – that being tucked away for a while can bring life, that there are blessings contained within. However, I discovered as I grew older that those hidden alone times were something I still hungered for but seemed also to bring a slight tinge of feeling lonely and lost, and I became less keen to pursue them. However, I realised as a new Christian that the missing element had of course been to share it with my heavenly Dad. He showed me that if I invite Him into that space too, it becomes a time of restoration in my innermost self, a time of feeling not lost and alone, but wonderfully loved and found by my Best Friend and King. When you look at it like that, choosing to take your time out with Him is a bit of a no-brainer!!

And yet, as I discovered, I can understand the need for it, have revelation on the significance of it, yearn for the fruit from it – and still struggle with the doing of it! You see, with the Urban Retreat, God has provided in a very practical and physical way, an aid to our drawing closer to Him in the busyness of life. As a space dedicated to time out with the Lord, it has, amongst many things, creative prayer aids, tranquil spots and soaking spaces, a meditative trail and pointers to the Lord. (It's so much more than I could have ever dreamed up or imagined – but that's our Daddy for you, isn't it?!) However, even though He comes and brings His beautiful presence to the place, sometimes the blocks and challenges to resting in Him come from within.

But the good news is that there is help! Again, God in His kindness not only knows what we need; He also provides for it. He puts us in community, with those both past and present, ancient and recent, to help us grow together and be blessed by following the paths that others have already walked. There are those who are a few steps further down the road in the practice of resting with the Lord, and we can learn from them. These are people who can guide us, encourage us, help us to identify the blocks and position ourselves for God to remove them, and to draw closer to the heart of our heavenly Dad. Simon Jones is one of those people. His insights and writings are given such depth, relevance and authenticity because he writes as one who walks it. It is also because he loves to draw wisdom from the wealth of the many others who have gone before. I believe that hanging out with God is as ancient a desire as any in man, and that as a result there are many ancient paths that have already been walked that can lead one there.

So I encourage you to be encouraged by Simon. Let the truths he has seen touch your heart and give you hope. May they unlock a deeper knowing of the Lord for you; may they help you put yourself in a place where He can draw you close to Himself. After all, He longs for that even more than you do! Stop, stand for a while and look. Ask for the good way, seek out those ancient paths, and may they lead you deeper into the Father's arms. And may you, amongst the many, many treasures which you will undoubtedly find, may you also find rest for your soul.

Hilary Garcia, Founder – The Urban Retreat

Prayer as living in God's love

Have you ever had that sensation where you say a familiar word a lot and it suddenly seems strange to you? Words are important to us, aren't they? Perhaps you have also had the experience where you had always assumed that a certain word meant one thing, and then found out that the dictionary definition was different to what you thought. We also have some effect ourselves on the meaning of words. I wonder what people first thought when the word 'wicked' suddenly began to be used to mean 'absolutely awesome' instead of 'extremely evil'. I remember people of older generations in the little church I grew up in disapproving of this particular language development! Certain words also evoke certain feelings in us, often due to experiences and preconceived ideas associated with that word. So it is with a word like 'prayer'. Every person hears that word according to all they have heard and experienced surrounding it throughout their life.

In this first reflection, I would like to look at the question of what prayer is. My feeling is that even though we may have been told differently and know differently, in the back of our minds we are all affected by a concept of prayer that is very focused on 'doing'. We may have let go of the idea that prayer is a shopping list, where we list off a number of things we want God to do for the day and then we sign off. Still, I feel, for most of us, we are somewhere between this and the true meaning of prayer.

Ask yourself for a moment how you see prayer. Do you connect prayer in your mind with the word 'intercession' (which is standing in the gap on behalf of others)? Now intercession is a wonderful thing for all of us to enter into at the leading of the Holy Spirit, and some people have a particular gift in this sort of prayer, but it is always a secondary aspect that flows out of true prayer in the heart. I would go as far as to say that like many words there is a sense in which the word 'prayer' has lost its original meaning, and consequently when we hear it something in us switches off. Could it also be our slightly faulty concepts that mean we can get to a time of prayer that we have set aside, but find we don't know where to start?

Even writing the word 'prayer' I feel a religiosity surrounding it, not because of the word itself, but because of what we have lost. There can be such a sense of 'I should', obligation and 'having to', that the thought of coming to be with God and spending time with Him seems like a burden.

What if we scrap all our previous concepts for a moment and turn to thoughts of our deepest heartfelt desires, whatever they may be? What if we think of our desperate need and longing to be loved by someone, to be accepted, to be liked? Perhaps, whether we are in a relationship or not, we could think of a passionate, intimate and tender love relationship with another human being – how does this make us feel? I expect the words 'should', 'obligation', 'have to', 'struggle' and 'boring' don't come into our minds when we think of this! What if such a love relationship is actually the heart of prayer? A passionate, intimate exchange of love between two lovers. The Song of Solomon is a beautiful picture of human love, but it also touches on the true nature of the love of God. Christian writers on prayer through the centuries, such as John of the Cross, Jeanne Guyon, and more recently Mike Bickle, have used it to capture the essence of prayer.

Maybe one of the reasons prayer can be hard is because, even if we have already accepted some of what I am saying, deep in the back of our minds we still associate prayer with 'doing', as I have been suggesting, and so it becomes yet another obligation to add to the day's already full schedule... yet another burden. But Jesus declared Himself to be the One who lifts burdens (Matthew 11:28), not the One who puts extra burdens on us! So why not release yourself from all obligation to pray, and see if you can hear His invitation to come, and enter more deeply into the greatest love relationship you've ever known, and the only relationship that can satisfy the deepest longings and fill the deepest caverns of your heart. You long for this, whether you are aware of that longing or not – God put the longing in every human being, and the more we taste of Him and His love, the more we long for Him.

I recently heard James Jordan of Fatherheart Ministries say:

I don't find it a hard command to allow myself to be loved. I find it a hard command to be obedient, to be disciplined, to spend hours on my knees ... I find that hard. But [I have realised] that prayer is just about receiving love ... First come into His presence, but remember Whose presence you're coming into. The Bible says God is love... so when we come to pray we're coming into His love. We've totally missed that.[1]

He is absolutely right. To be loved and let love pour into your soul is what prayer is all about – for we cannot even love God unless we've first experienced Him loving us (1 John 4:19).

And so why not ask your heart how you feel about prayer, if you see it in this way: something you don't have to do if you don't want to, but an invitation from the One who loves you more than you can imagine, an invitation to let Him love you in your actual experience and fulfil the deepest desires of your heart that no other human being (as good as human relationships are) could fill.

This is what we mean today by soaking, resting in prayer, or, as monastic communities have referred to it, 'contemplative prayer'. Being still is a very important part of this, though it is

---

[1] James Jordan, Father Heart School Finland 2010, teaching CDs produced by Father's House Finland.

not the only part. What is important is that this type of prayer is about 'communion', by which I mean *intimately connecting heart to heart with God and experiencing love flowing from Him to you and letting love flow back to Him*. Even when you may feel dry this can still be happening in the deepest places of your heart. In these days He is longing to show Himself as Father, our real Father who wants to be a father to us and pour His father-love through our hearts, healing our deepest wounds. He is also showing us in this place that we can be a bride to His Son Jesus and enter into the greatest love affair the world has ever seen. The invitation is there for us if we so desire!

Even when we begin to see prayer in this way, it does not mean we experience no resistance in us to it, for our wounded hearts can often want to run from a God who simply wants to love us. Still, it is my belief that if we do begin to see prayer like this, we will experience an intense longing for it.

May you find yourself longing for the presence of your loving Father like never before.

Knowing Father

A single word can make a difference to our reading of a whole book... such is the power of words. If we miss the meaning of that one important word it could affect our understanding of the whole book. Just as wrongly understanding one word could alter the meaning of a whole book, the way a word, sentence or phrase is spoken can also totally alter its meaning. I think we often totally misread the Scriptures because we are not hearing them as they were spoken. If we could see the smile, the look of compassion, or the loving touch that often accompanied the words of Jesus it would radically affect how we receive them.

It is like this with our understanding of our relationship to God as Father. You can't have been in a Christian church or group for long before you heard God referred to as Father, whether through the Lord's prayer or through teaching about 'God the Father'. However, this can be far removed from knowing Him *fathering us in our hearts*, even though the words themselves may not have changed that much. In this reflection, I would like to write a little about the revelation of the Father – it is central to how we will experience our times of prayer.

Throughout Christian history it would be fair to say that there has been a theology of 'God the Father', but for most of our history there has been very little experience of relating to him *as Father*... In these days this is, I believe, the most profound revelation the Holy Spirit is giving us, calling us back to something almost untouched since perhaps the first century of Christianity: And when we see it, it changes absolutely everything!

Consider the difference between saying, 'God is your Father' if you believe this in some sort of rational, 'accepting the truth of the statement' kind of way, and then the words of God in 2 Corinthians 6:18: 'I will *be a Father to you*, and you will be my sons and daughters'.[2] Stop and consider these words for a moment – 'I will *be a Father to you*...' This means He is not just 'God the Father', and He doesn't just want us to pray 'Our Father' in some general sense... He actually wants to *be* a Father to you... directly... to father you in your heart, and to heal and fill in all the gaps from all that was painful and missing in your own relationship with your father. Even beyond simply healing your past, He wants to father you in a way that you had never dreamt was possible.

You see, if Jesus is the eternally begotten Son of God, it means that He has always been the Son, and therefore His Father has always been Father. It is not some distant analogy, as has often been thought. He is not just *like a father* – He *is* Father! As James Jordan puts it, 'He's even more Father than He is Creator – Creator is what He does, Father is who He is!'[3] And as Father He loves you with the same love He has for Jesus. Jack Winter, one of the first people to really grasp this revelation in recent years,[4] asked Him about this one day. He said, 'Father, how can you love us as much as you love Jesus? Jesus was perfect.'

In reply, Father said words to the effect of, 'Yes, but I don't love Him because He is perfect; I love Him because He is my Son!'[5] And so it is for you!

This brings fresh light for us on Matthew 18:1-3:

---

[2] Italics added.

[3] I've often heard James say this in talks. This is summed up well in his book, *Sonship* (Taupo, New Zealand: Tree of life Media, 2012), p78.

[4] Jack Winter founded Daystar Ministries and received a profound revelation of the Father's love.

[5] http://www.fatherheart.tv/father-himself-loves-you (accessed 22nd April 2014). Jack was one of the first people to see that the Father's love is a reality, which can be imparted. People don't need to just be told that the Father loves them, they need to encounter His love in their hearts.

At that time the disciples came to Jesus and asked, 'Who is the greatest in the kingdom of heaven?'

He called a little child and had him stand among them. And he said, 'I tell you the truth, unless you change and become like little children you will never enter the kingdom of heaven.'

And so, once we can accept that we are really little boys and girls who just need to be loved, our prayer life is transformed – we experience more of the kingdom of heaven.

I have read many books on prayer and taken a lot of good from most of them, but I can say that wherever they have missed this central reality of the Father, to one degree or another prayer has become a 'work'. When you see who the Father is, prayer is about coming and sitting on His lap and letting Him love you and loving Him back. We have known that Jesus is the Way, but have we known that He is the Way to the Father... to *our* Father... your Father, my Father, Abba... who actually likes us as we are? Pretty cool, hey?

We're all on a journey to seeing more of this. None of us has yet arrived. May the Holy Spirit open our eyes to see this!

Vulnerable and fragile, yet so, so beautiful

I recently had the privilege of going on an individually guided retreat in silence for eight days at St Beuno's, a Christian retreat centre in North Wales. It was quite amusing at times watching people attempting to eat their meals in silence! The Lord very clearly took me on a journey during this time to show me that He was calling me to love and accept my vulnerability, fragility and weakness. I saw that Jesus came as a vulnerable baby and died for us in a full expression of vulnerability before us... I saw that all that exists, from a flower swaying in the wind to the earth 'hanging' in the middle of space, is vulnerable and fragile... and only is what it is by the loving, protective hand of the Father.

Perhaps you, like me, have found this a difficult truth to accept: *that it's ok to be weak, and it's ok not to have it all together.* Paul got this: 'For Christ's sake, I delight in weaknesses' (2 Corinthians 12:10). How many of us could honestly say the same? So often our Christianity has become focused around becoming strong, competent, equipped, skilled, able and confident, leaving us little space to be ourselves, to be who we really are. Constantly we feel like we have to 'be something'. And the world around us encourages us into this too.

I work in a Christian retreat centre called the Urban Retreat. We have a beautiful roof garden. Earlier in the year I was sitting in this garden reading through the Beatitudes. We have often heard them taught as eight good virtues to acquire in order to be an effective Christian. Suddenly, as I was sitting there, I saw in a fresh way that the first one, 'Blessed are the poor in spirit' (Matthew 5:3), really sums up the rest: those who know they don't have anything, have everything... that is really what Jesus is saying.

Jesus Himself lived this life: the life of a little dependent child. He said, 'The Son can do nothing by himself' (John 5:19).

Nothing... No thing... He said it was the Father speaking through Him and working through Him. Bill Johnson points out that Jesus couldn't do a miracle; He couldn't heal a single sick person.[6]

The same is true of us. 'Apart from me you can do nothing', He told His disciples (John 15:5). No thing. Ask yourself: Can you heal the sick? Can you love the unlovely? Can you speak the word of God? No! Only 'Christ in you, the hope of glory' (Colossians 1:27) makes this possible, only as we live out of the same dependent relationship He had with His Daddy. We don't become like Jesus by human effort, but by having the same intimate relationship He had with His Father.

Last year in Northern Ireland I heard one of the funniest and most countercultural messages I have ever heard. A guy called Jeff was basically saying that all God needs is our incompetence – he exhorted us to be incompetent for God! In other words, to realise that we cannot do anything... Little children are, in this sense of the word, 'incompetent', but do we criticise them for it and tell them to sort themselves out? No, we love them for it!

You are a beautiful, beloved, infinitely valuable child of God. You are also a little child who is weak and completely unable to work unless God works through you. This really takes off all the pressure of having to perform and it allows us to accept ourselves as we are (it also happens to mean that God can do absolutely anything through us!).

I am still on a journey to accepting my vulnerability and not feeling the pressure to be strong, but I have begun to see that the places where we are most vulnerable and weak are the very places in our hearts that God declares as so, so beautiful.

---

[6] Bill Johnson, *When Heaven Invades Earth* (Shippensburg: Treasure House, an imprint of Destiny Image Publishers, Inc, 2003), p29. In other words, everything He did, He did as a dependent child in the power of the Holy Spirit.

Sleeping on a cushion

I was struck recently by the story in Mark 4 where a storm comes up on the Sea of Galilee and the disciples panic and accuse the sleeping Jesus, saying, 'Don't you care if we drown?' (Mark 4:38). He gets up, gently reminds them of their lack of faith, and calms the storm.

I allowed my imagination to see the events happening with myself as another disciple (using your imagination to see the events happening can be a really helpful way to enter into Scripture, and a good way to find out your own heart responses). I then, to my surprise, found myself accusing Jesus from somewhere deep down in my heart, 'Why do you always leave when things get hard?'

You don't realise these things are in your heart until you see them!

The Lord was touching a deep place in me and I realised that I needed to go back to this story and see what the Lord wanted to show me there. The next day when I read it again I was struck by the fact that Jesus was *sleeping on a cushion* (Mark 4:38).[7] I had always known that in this story He was sleeping, but somehow I had missed that He was sleeping on a cushion! It's funny how one small phrase can make a massive difference, and what it made me realise was how at rest He was, even in the midst of a raging storm. What was the secret He had discovered? It was having His Father's chest to lie on, and to rest, sleep and live on in the midst of all that was going on around Him. He was truly at rest.

The story, as it speaks to our hearts, goes way beyond the physical conditions, and makes us think of the storms of our own hearts and lives – our present fears and worries; situations beyond our control that we would never have chosen; difficulty

---

[7] Italics added.

with things that are a part of normal life; grief and loss; pain, abuse and loneliness when we were young... Whatever they are, perhaps if we look into the heart of Jesus and why He is sleeping, we will see that He never leaves us – even in the storms – *and He never left you* when you were a child and things were really hard for you, when you felt alone, or didn't get all the love you needed, or perhaps were hurt really badly. He never leaves; He is the perfect representation of His Father who is a perfect Father – always lovingly with us.

So why, you may say, does it sometimes feel like He is not there at the hardest moments I experience in life? Why sometimes when I pray does He feel far away, even though I desire to be with Him?

Perhaps the secret is that He has not gone anywhere... He is just sleeping on a cushion. Therese of Lisieux, a nun from the nineteenth century who was a complete legend in my opinion, said words to the effect of – When Jesus is sleeping in the boat of my life, I just let Him sleep. I don't try and wake Him![8] In other words, we can be comfortable with His presence even in the moments He feels distant. The fact He is sleeping doesn't mean He has abandoned us or is angry with us, but rather that He loves us and is comfortable enough with our presence to fall asleep!

None of this means that He doesn't care about what we go through – He is overflowing with compassion and feels our pain more intensely and deeply than we do ourselves... but what it does mean is that He knows, whatever the storm, that everything is ultimately going to be ok! As Julian of Norwich, an anchoress from the fourteenth century, said, 'All shall be well, and all shall be well, and all manner of thing shall be

---

[8] I've paraphrased a couple of things she said, quoted in James McCaffrey, *The Fire of Love: Praying with Therese of Lisieux* (Norfolk: Canterbury Press, 1998), p64.

well.'[9] Perhaps, instead of accusing Him like I did, and like the disciples did, we could grab a cushion, lie down and join Him, 'sleeping' through our own storms and those raging around us, trusting that we have a Father who is taking care of every detail of our lives for us.

And, by the way, if you take some time out to pray and find that you fall asleep, you are not being unspiritual – it's just that you need to rest!!

---

[9] Robert Llewellyn (ed.), *Enfolded in Love: Daily Readings with Julian of Norwich* (London: Darton, Longman and Todd Ltd, 2009), p23.

He just wants you for you

I recently returned from spending a week in a cabin in Wales, right by a stream, owned by a couple of friends. The only noise was the sound of the stream, the wind, the rain and the occasional animal. After four and a half days, I came to a sudden realisation – that actually, I had come with a list of all that I wanted God to sort out in my life, and my many thoughts about different ways these things could be worked out, but all He wanted was just to be with me... for me... not for how sorted or healed I was, not for where I'd got to on my journey with Him, not for any holiness I'd achieved, but just for me, as I was... as I am.

Forgive me; I know it sounds basic! After seven years of going away and doing this sort of thing, it took *me* by surprise that Father brought me right back to what it's all about. Sometimes you think you already know something. I mean, I've got past bringing actual lists when I come to be with Him, but I realised that internally I had... a list... a certain amount of things I wanted to get healed and dealt with ready for the next stage of my life.

But His thoughts are higher than ours... His ways are not our ways... (Isaiah 55:8-9)

Let me ask you: how many times do you come to God with a list, whether material or internal, of 'Let's get this done today Lord', or 'Let's deal with this issue.' I think, in different ways, we all do.

But in that moment looking down the Welsh valley, I knew, I just knew – the Lord didn't even need to use words to tell me; I could just sense His heart – His heart was saying, 'Actually Simon, you know what? I really love you, and I just want us to have some time together... just being, with no other purpose than to simply love each other... to walk, rest and sit together.' It's as if this is all that really matters to the Lord!

Later that day, as I was sitting in His presence, looking at the wooden cross over the stream from the cabin, the tears started flowing. It was the thought, *'He just wants me for me'*, that was going deep into my soul. I found myself thinking, 'I don't think I've ever been loved like this.' Nothing I could do or bring, or get sorted, is what He wants to love about me – He just wants to love me.

He was inviting me back into the intimacy Adam and Eve had in the Garden of Eden... the intimacy of just being with each other, and being with their Father... of being together. Yes, ruling over creation, but only in the context of this intimacy. He was showing me what He really wanted from me, and inviting me also to just want Him for Him, not for anything He could do for me or achieve in me, but simply for Himself... God... as He is! This really is the heart of God – that we are loved for who we are, and this enables us to love Him for who He is.

So, when you come into His presence, there is an invitation, if you would like to take it up, to be wanted for who you are, to be pursued by God for your heart... your very essence... not for your ability to produce, or to be sorted. And an invitation to let the desire in you grow for His very nature, His very being – to come into a deep experience of oneness, of union with Him.

Actually, as it turned out, on the final day, the seventh day of the week, God healed a very deep root in me, but it had happened by us just enjoying each other's company, not so much for any words we could speak to each other or any things we could do for each other, but just for the sake of being together. And for you... whatever needs healing in your life, God is faithful to do it, but He invites you to not worry about any of that stuff and let His timing be His timing. Just enjoy Him... loving you now! You are so perfect and precious in His eyes as you are now!

Oh, and in case you're asking about the fruit, the holiness, the 'changing the world'; seeing people saved, delivered, healed; the getting anointed, the getting equipped and releasing giftings... Well, you could seek after those things, or you could look at John 15, and choose to abide in the Vine... IN the vine... IN Jesus... heart to heart... in close fellowship, and allow all those things to be 'added unto you' (Matthew 6:33, KJV). If fruit needs to grow it just will in this place. When intimacy becomes a priority the fruit can't help but grow; you don't have to try and grow it. I've never heard a branch saying, 'I'm just not going to grow apples today.' If it stays connected to the tree, the apples are simply going to grow and grow well. You don't even have to try and cultivate or keep the fruit that grows, for the Father is the Gardener! (John 15:1)

I had one prayer come out of my heart in this time: two weeks before going I had heard that Heidi Baker was saying there was a call to be 'in the Heart of God' – not just near to it, not just connected to it, but right inside it: *in His heart*... So my prayer, as God was showing me all this, became, 'Father, take me right into Your heart and leave me there...' And then I would sit with Him... in silence.

My friend Solveig, who used to work with me at the retreat, drew a beautiful picture of someone walking towards a big golden heart in the setting of a garden. I would love you to see the picture. Perhaps you are able to imagine that image...

May you hear the call to walk right into His heart and discover there that *He just wants you for you*!

Silence is golden

A journalist once asked Mother Teresa, 'What do you say when you pray to God?'

Her answer took him by surprise – 'Nothing,' she said.

Recovering himself, and thinking he was catching her drift, he said, 'Well ok then, when you pray, what does God say to you?'

'Nothing,' she said, leaving him speechless.

I heard this story recounted by Tony Campolo years ago. He quite rightly pointed out that the most intimate moments between lovers are actually when words of love themselves are not enough... gazing into each other's eyes, embracing and quietly being together can go even deeper than words.

Words are central to our faith – Jesus is the Word of God, the Bible is God's inspired word of love to us and we know that the world only exists because God spoke the 'word' to create it and it was done. But before He spoke, He was...

There are many biblical pictures of silence: the call in Psalm 37:7 to 'be still before the Lord', or the picture in Psalm 131 of a weaned child at its mother's breast, stilled and quieted... at peace, no need for words... learning to trust.

We live in a world so full of words, activity and noise that we have come to see silence as something to be escaped and avoided at all costs (and often, of course, there are reasons for this – for all our own pains and needs become a lot more obvious when the noise lessens) – but silence is not emptiness, as we have thought. Why is it, if you go into the heart of the wilderness, the valley, the mountain top, the woods or the desert, that you will 'hear' silence? Perhaps silence is not actually nothing, but is in fact the sound of God's love being imparted to all that is made. Perhaps, if we wait long enough in the silence, we will find ourselves immersed in this love.

Words are good; words from God are even better. After a dramatic encounter with God and an experience of freedom in December 2002, I experienced six and a half years where God spoke to me in words as regularly as someone with whom you would live with as husband or wife. I spoke and He spoke back. He still speaks, but the last few years have been different: it hasn't really been through words. At first I struggled and battled to work out what was wrong and to get those words back from Him. You see, I'm a words person – it's one of my love languages. I like having God speak words into my spirit like a gentle whisper of love... But during more recent times, particularly, I have had my eyes opened... and I have begun to see that while God loves to speak to us like that, some of the deepest communication we will ever have with Him is wordless. Sometimes, in the silence, we will experience that there is a love that goes right into the depths of our spirit – deeper than words can communicate. This is 'silent communion', oneness – there are times within this when we feel very little, but yet at a deep level can be communing with God.

And so, I would like to say to you – if you are experiencing many words, pictures and visions from God, then wonderful – ask for more! 'For everyone who has, will be given more' (Matthew 25:29). But if, when you come to pray and be with God, all you experience is dryness, restlessness, emptiness, silence... don't give up; don't think God is angry with you or that He is punishing you; don't believe the lie that He is distant; and don't think it's you – that you can't hear, that you can't receive. No, stay with the silence. Stay there... Be silent, be still, let your God love you. Listen to Him in and through the silence – it is the sound of His love for you.

And, I believe, in this He takes us to a deeper place of trust. For, if we only know that He is loving us when we are experiencing Him in a particular way, then we are dependent on that experience. If, however, we know that even in the silence we are being held by the everlasting arms, we will be as confident of the love of God when we feel very little as when we are inebriated with overflowing emotions. For, ultimately, the Father's love is not received in our emotions, minds or wills, though it may touch them; it is received in our hearts. The love of God, as James Jordan says, 'wraps around our spirit',[10] and we just know, because we know, because we know we are loved.

John of the Cross knew about the touches of God in the spirit very well, where one could not really perceive God with the 'senses' as he called them, and yet at the same time could know that one's spirit was being drawn into a deep encounter with love. The unknown author of the book *The Cloud of Unknowing* also had an idea about this. He spoke of a silent longing love for God. He saw that, as valuable as many other experiences of God could be, in contemplation one could be led into a place where it is not really the words or revelations of God that are given to the believer, but God himself!

So, in the presence of His love...
  Why not –
    Be silent,
    Be still,
      Breathe His love in deep.
  Whisper His name –
    Jesus... Jesus...
    Father... Father...
    Spirit...
  And let your mind become still –
    And wait... and wait...
      In the silence...

---

[10] Heard on a teaching CD.

You may experience dazzling lights, visions and words, or you may just experience silence... but perhaps you will come to see that silence is golden... for you are resting right inside the heart of God.

God is not angry with you

You believe that God is love and that God loves you. I'm sure of it. But let me be bold – what do you mean by it? And how deep is it in your heart? Let's test the waters...

What if I said to you: God is not angry with you... Not only is He not angry with you today, but He never was angry with you, and He never will be angry with you... there is absolutely nothing you could ever do to make Him angry with you... Why? Because He is completely head over heels in love with the very core of who you are and who He made you to be...

Then, I think a good percentage of people would start to think about certain Old Testament passages and even New Testament passages that seem to suggest otherwise. Many would think of the Christian teaching they've heard throughout their lives, and others would think of their experiences of parents and other authority figures who were easily angered.

The Bible says God is 'slow to anger' (Psalm 103:8; Exodus 34:6). It's not easy to make Him angry... Yet for many years religion has depicted exactly the opposite so that people live 'holy' lives in fear of God's anger.

So why have we believed this lie? I think it's the glasses we've been looking through. For so long we have been taught about the wrath of God and we've lived in a world full of angry people, that I think when we come to the Bible we look through those glasses. Therefore, when we hear anger in the Scriptures, we have internalised that to mean God will be angry with me if I make a big mistake. But why don't we take the glasses off for a moment and step into a world which is about a Father so in love with His creation, with His sons and daughters, that when He saw the suffering they created for themselves He was willing to give the life of His beloved Son for them. That changes things! (And don't think it was only Jesus who suffered on the cross... in some senses the Father's suffering was at least as great. Most parents would rather suffer themselves than see their children suffer – this was a great sacrifice.) It's like putting a clearer pair of glasses on. When we look through *those* glasses, we see the opposite of what we thought was true. His anger was only ever with the way sin was destroying and tearing apart the precious kids that He loved... but He never felt that towards them – it was an expression of His love for them!! And so, in that love, He took that thing which was destroying them and removed it once and for all – so you can know that your sin has been taken away forever. But He never was angry with us in the first place; all He ever felt and all He ever feels *towards us* for our sin is compassion for why we do what we do.

You see, if you have any part of you that feels that, while God might be love, you can never be totally sure that He won't suddenly become angry with you, then it is really hard to relax in His presence and let Him love you. It will be a block to intimacy with Him... simply because, although your mind may choose to come to pray, your heart is scared to come close, even when you're sitting in His presence. Our hearts just don't want to come close to somebody who might get angry with us – that's how we've been wired. It's tenderness that draws us into someone's heart... If you could feel the gentleness and tenderness in His heart right now I guarantee that you would be drawn towards it.

In 2003, at a time when He was revealing a lot about His grace to me, the Father spoke into my spirit one day and said, 'I delight in you, even when I don't delight in the things you do.' It caused me to stop and think... Is that really true...? Can it really be true...? Ok, maybe minor things won't stop Him delighting in me, but what if I were to do the worst things I could imagine doing? Surely then He would be angry with me rather than delighting in me? One day, soon after this, I was reading Jeremiah, a book full of God speaking against the actions of the Israelites, when I discovered this verse:

> Is not Ephraim my dear son, the child in whom I delight?
> Though I often speak against him, I still remember him.
> Therefore my heart yearns for him; I have great compassion
> for him.
> *Jeremiah 31:20*

And I saw clearly that God's delight was still in Israel, even though His child was as far away as he could be from God's purpose for him.

For too long our glasses have said that God is loving and Father on the one hand but holy and judge on the other. We have split his nature into two parts... Christian history, from Early Church Father, Tertullian (who was a lawyer) onwards, has understood salvation in the context of a courtroom... But the problem is it's really hard to take your shoes off, don your slippers, curl up and relax with a judge. If the true nature and personality of God was judge, He would have sent a member of the courtroom to show the world what He was really like. He didn't! His ultimate revelation of Himself was by sending a Son. If it's a Son whom He sent to show what He was really like in His heart, then in His heart, His essence, He must be a loving Father. Jesus said, 'The Father judges no one, but has entrusted all judgment to the Son' (John 5:22). He also said of Himself, 'I did not come to judge the world, but to save it' (John 12:47).

Anchoress Julian of Norwich had some amazing revelations of Jesus, and she was one of the few people in church history bold enough to say, 'I saw no whit of anger in God – in short or in long term.'[11] She also said that He spoke to her, 'So kindly

---

[11] Robert Llewellyn (ed.), *In Love Enclosed: More Daily Readings with Julian of Norwich* (London: Darton, Longman and Todd Ltd, 2004), p72.

and without a hint of blame'.[12] She spent most of her life resting in Him, so she should know!

Don't you see?
God is for you not against you.
He wants you to come close.
His heart is full of tender love for you.
It really is safe to come near...

You can take your shoes off, sit in front of the fire, curl up and relax in the presence of your loving Father, in His house...

There's not going to be any anger coming at you... ever. Oh yes, He just happens to be awesome, holy, perfect, Almighty God, a King... He can't help it! But He wants YOU to know Him as Dad.

---

[12] Llewellyn, *In Love Enclosed*, p46.

Taking a retreat

Have you ever found yourself wishing for more, after spending an hour or two with our Father? His presence can have that effect on us! Have you ever found yourself thinking, 'This is great, but I just feel like I need longer with God, longer to process, more space, peace and silence, more time just to be'? If these are thoughts you've been having, I would really encourage you to listen to them, for they are the longing of your heart. Why not book a retreat somewhere in the UK (or elsewhere, if you don't live in the UK), where you can stay overnight? You might have to face 1,000 reasons why it is not practical to do this, but perhaps the benefits will outweigh the seeming inconvenience.

Think of it – there are many Christian places around the country specifically designed to provide people with the space they long for simply to 'be', and yet many of us feel it is impossible to jump off the busy and noisy bus of life and make space for what our souls need. Often these places are reasonably priced and many simply suggest donations, which means if you can't afford what is asked for you give what you can!

I'm not saying everyone should do this. We are all different – each of us is designed uniquely by God. Some are more 'active'; some are more 'contemplative'. I do believe we all need some space and solitude in our lives, but not everyone may desire to go away for a retreat. However, I expect that many of you would be wired in one way or another to love this kind of experience – so I just want to offer encouragement and a couple of tips, if the Lord is stirring you. It would be great to see the Lord take people away to encounter Him and then bring the riches of these encounters back into what He is doing in our local areas.

What is a retreat?

It is a time period set aside for intimacy with God, usually staying somewhere for at least one or two nights, so that it becomes a period of time with God, rather than simply a time of prayer.

Though it is not quite the same as a holiday, it may include many of the same elements, such as getting good sleep, rest, and eating well. Depending on how the Spirit leads you, you may also choose to include recreational activities, such as walks, reading for relaxation and creativity... It's just that generally you are alone and the focus when you start your time is to be led into a place of deep rest and love within the heart of God.

What are the benefits?

Rest; finding out that God loves you as you are and that He is your Father; an awakening to the presence of God; a growing knowledge of His voice and leading; inner healing from hurts; journeying to find your true self in these times; space to think; space just to be; release of creativity; receiving of revelation; joy; being enabled to give yourself more fully and to be more present once you are back and around others.

Where do I take one?

I would highly recommend going somewhere where there is some sort of countryside as this tends to really help the soul appreciate God's beauty and find a context for peace. (See the end of the reflection for suggestions of how to find a retreat that suits you.)

There are different sorts of experience available – some are in the context of a community, where you are around others but still have your own room, and at others the experience is close to total solitude. There are many where you can go and simply do your own thing, and others with someone to guide you through the time. It is worth considering what you need.

I would say though, be discerning and let the Lord lead you. Some Christian retreats have embraced, within what they do, certain eastern practices and yoga, as well as some elements of secular psychology which might also be unhelpful. However, don't limit yourself to only what is in your own part of the body of Christ – some of my deepest experiences of God have come in retreat centres which were outside of my own part of the body.

How long should I go for?

Do what is right for you. Start smaller and build up. If at any stage you have no desire for more, then stop there. That is what is right for you at that time.

My suggestion, if you have never done this before, is to test the calling by taking a whole day somewhere, such as a nearby retreat or a solitary place in the countryside and see how you find that.

Then I would suggest booking two or three nights. One night is better than nothing, but it doesn't give you the restfulness of having a full day away. Three nights (which gives you two full days) could be the optimum to start with as it often takes the first day to recover, but at the same time it is not too long.

In the long term, a week can be a good period of time as this allows time to really wind down into resting in God, but this is not right for everyone.

What do I do when I'm there?

In one sense this is a really good question; in another sense it's a slightly silly one. It's sort of like saying, 'What do I do when I'm on honeymoon with my husband or wife?' Ultimately no one can tell you how to spend your time with God. However, as some practical suggestions might help, here they are:

- Unless God calls you to fast, then eat well, as you will need the energy for encountering Him, though you may well choose to eat simply. Cooking and eating can be really blessed times in the presence of God.

- Sleep well – it's a lot harder to listen and receive from God when you are exhausted! I suggest not setting your alarm and letting God give you the sleep you need – when you need to wake up, you will.

- I know it sounds funny to say, but eating and sleeping could be the two main activities of your retreat! In that, if your heart so desires it, you may just want to sit and look out of the window when you are awake and simply be with God! That is ok!

- Of course, have your Bible and a notepad available. Journaling is great for these times, and the Scriptures can be used to give a backbone to your retreat. But don't feel guilty if you don't read the Bible as much as you expect to!

- Walking can be really good for listening to Him... and just enjoying life and nature! But don't be surprised if you end up taking whole days without going outside.

- Space for creativity often plays a part, and art and crafts stuff can be great to take.

- So can spiritual reading, or even recreational reading – you don't always have to do 'spiritual' things on a retreat!

- On the other hand, all these can be a distraction. I tend to read quite a lot on retreats, but last year a nun helped me see that even this can be a distraction from the silence and being... Let your heart lead.

- Don't be surprised or discouraged if it takes a long time to focus. The mind can still be busy even after the body has started to rest. There are lots of suggestions in Christian books on contemplative prayer of ways to still your mind and focus on Father in prayer, such as using the imagination or quietly repeating Scripture... All these may help and are worth looking at, but ultimately the key is to accept yourself as you are, to be, and to believe that in time all will become restful within.

- Some personality types may prefer a more structured way of using their time. There are many helpful models of planning the day, such as some within Celtic spirituality which structure in space for prayer, reading, silence, creativity, relaxation and Scripture. However, if you do prefer this I would recommend leaving in space for spontaneity, as the Spirit loves freedom. Don't be boxed in by what seems acceptable to others – the Lord may even lead you to have a whole day in bed! The horizontal position is the place of visions and dreams, after all!

- You may experience dazzling lights and feel like you are in a place thick with His manifest presence – enjoy it if you do! Having said this, a friend who helps people through retreats often says don't be discouraged if you don't see or hear anything when you are on retreat! God often works in hidden ways, hiding things in the heart – you may not know fully what you have received until you come back home and are among people again. I found this advice hard to understand at first, but over the years it has made more sense to me.

- Don't go too focused on what needs sorting in your life – God is much more interested in just being with you, and He is more than able to bring something up to heal if He wants to. Yes, it can sometimes be helpful to start your time by saying to Jesus what it is you want Him to do for you, but I would say the more you can look at the time as a blank page for God to write on, the better!

I hope this helps and encourages those of you whom God is calling to try it out.

(For finding a retreat: You may find The Retreat Association helpful for UK retreats: http://www.retreats.org.uk/[13] If you click on 'Home' and then 'Find a Retreat' you will be able to search for retreats by areas of the UK. This is a really good resource. However, I would say, if you can go somewhere on a personal recommendation, it is often the best thing, and also that there are some 'gems' which don't advertise themselves through a website.)

---

[13] Accessed 23rd April 2014.

You are more than you think you are

Do you realise that when God looks at you He sees a depth of beauty and glory within you that you cannot even begin to imagine? I was talking about this with some friends recently. It's well known in psychology circles that we only see part of ourselves. There are the open parts everyone we meet sees, the partially veiled parts those who know us see, and then the hidden parts only those closest to us see. Deeper than this is that which a husband or wife can see, and then the part of us known only to ourselves and God... But beyond all this, there is a depth to us that even we have no idea about, and are in a process of discovering.

Thomas Merton writes:

The secret of my identity is hidden in the love and mercy of God ... Therefore, there is only one problem on which all my existence, my peace and my happiness depend: to discover myself in discovering God. If I find him I will find myself, and if I find my true self I will find him.[14]

Listen as well to John's words:

Dear friends now we are children of God, and what we will be has not yet been made known. But we know that when he appears, we shall be like him, for we shall see him as he is.
1 John 3:2

So... there's more to be found: *'What we will be has not yet been made known'!* The question is: when we see Him as He is, are we going to become something we are not now? In other words,

---

[14] Thomas Merton, *New Seeds of Contemplation* (London: Burns and Oates, a Continuum imprint, 2002), p34.

will we be different people? I don't believe we will. Yes, we will look different... but why? Because we will see Him more fully and therefore we will see who we are more fully, and so will others. So that means your journey is not to become something else, but rather to become more and more who you already are... more and more yourself!! You are that person now – it's just that you don't see it all yet, as God is in a process of uncovering your true identity (with a lot of love and healing on the way!).

Ok, so if your journey to become more like Jesus is actually a journey to be more yourself, then who are you?

Well, let's start with a few things – *You are an amazing, beautiful, loveable, awesome, special, wonderful child of God... You are incredible.* This might make you blush, but it's the truth, it really is! He rejoices over you with singing (Zephaniah 3:17). His good thoughts about you are as countless as the sand on the seashore (Psalm 139:18). Essentially, when He looks at you He says, 'Wow! Look at what I made.' Like any artist marvelling at the artwork he created, your Father is overwhelmed by your beauty!

For me I was helped to see the depth of beauty in who I am when I heard James Jordan talk about how God is our real Father (you see, I can't discover who I am unless I know who He is). He spoke about the fact that we are *more* than adopted sons and daughters. Adoption is a wonderful New Testament metaphor of the 'choosing love' of the Father, but if we stop there we miss the fullness of the revelation. Lots of areas of revelation work like this. There is a wonderful truth which you may discover first, and then an even more wonderful one, without which you would miss out: for example, if we only have the revelation that God has forgiven our sins, but we don't go on to the revelation that we have actually been given His righteous nature so that we are not sinful any more, then we miss something wonderful!

Well, similarly, if we stop at knowing we are 'adopted', we always feel like we came from somewhere else. An adopted child always has a sense that they came from somewhere else... but with our Father we came from Him – everything you are came from Him. You are His love conception. He thought about you and planned how He wanted you to be. He breathed into you the breath of life, knitting you together in your mother's womb!! Everything you are inside is as you were meant to be! You see, the overwhelming image of salvation in the New Testament is that of 'redemption'. When you redeem something you buy back what was already yours. Sin was never the deepest reality of who you were, even before you knew Jesus. You belonged to God. You came from Him, but you were lost and so He brought you back... So on the inside you are pure, lovely and beautiful, because everything you are came from Him... and He is pure beauty!!

When I first heard this, I felt as if every part of my soul suddenly had a rootedness it had not had before, knowing where I really came from. It really set me on a journey to liking who I am and who God made me to be. My wife and I were talking recently about a friend of ours who says that he likes everything about himself – that there's nothing he doesn't like. We talked about how free this makes you! People who like and accept themselves know how to play! They are great fun to be around. After a lot of journeying, I can now say from the depth of my heart that I like who I am too! I like all the uniqueness that God has put in me, and there's still more to discover.

Beloved of God... may you grow to like yourself more, as you discover more of who you are – a beautiful 'true' Son or Daughter – of our amazing Dad! You are more than you think you are!!

How can God like me when I sin?

I spoke a little about liking ourselves in the last reflection. Now, I want to look at one of the things that often makes us feel unlikeable. Let me ask you a question: How much on a scale of 1–10 would you say you like yourself? Reflect on the question honestly in your heart for a moment.

I'm guessing that a lot of people didn't come up with a 10. Perhaps you struggle with this? Perhaps deep down you feel that it's your sin that makes you unlikeable. I want to suggest two simple thoughts which I think can make a difference in this area:

1. God doesn't like you because of what you do or don't do, but because He is love.
2. Not only is He love, but you are also loveable on the inside.

1. God likes you independently of what you do

How many of us feel that if we do the right things, we are more acceptable to others than if we do the wrong things? Often the best human attempts at love can be conditional. This can cause us to think that God's love is too – but you see, God loves you as you are, not as you should be.

One of the most helpful Scriptures, I think, in demonstrating this is Romans 5:8 – 'God demonstrates his own love for us in this: *While we were still sinners*, Christ died for us.'[15]

Essentially, this tells me what God's love is like – He didn't love me when I had it all together; He came to me when I was the most lost, in the biggest mess, and furthest away from Him... At that point, He loved me just the same as He does

---

[15] Italics added.

now. At the lowest points of human history He loves even the biggest offender just the same as He does the biggest saint! You can't fit that into your mind, can you? But then, *grace* is topsy-turvy, after all!

2. You are loveable on the inside

Ok, so you may get to this point and be able to say, 'Ok, well God's love for me is unconditional, but that's about Him. He's good, He's loving... but I am still awful, sinful and unloveable – He loves me because of how good He is.' So, you still can't like yourself.

And that's where I think we miss the full mystery of what God has done for us. Scripture says, *'As far as the east is from the west, so far has he removed our transgressions from us'* (Psalm 103:12).[16] How far is the east from the west? Well, I don't think that Scripture is meant to cause us to come up with a distance in so many millions of miles!! How do you measure it? No, the point is it's infinite!! Removed an infinite distance! If your sins have been removed, this means you don't have them any more.

A lot of us can just about believe this for our past sins that we have copiously repented of, but would struggle much more to believe it for our present and future sins. When you read, 'He forgave us *all our sins*, having cancelled the written code, with its regulations, that was against us and that stood opposed to us; he took it away nailing it to the cross' – what does it make you think? (Colossians 2:13-14).[17] ALL OUR SINS can't just mean our past ones. This is talking about a 'once for all' action (Hebrews 9:26). Consider this: your sins – past, present and future – have been forgiven and taken away! All that is left is

---

[16] Italics added.
[17] Italics added.

the pure child of God that you were always intended to be even before you knew Jesus. You're a new creation, now!

I know we're broken vessels and need a lot of love to bring us a lot of healing. I know we make mistakes. But none of this changes who we are! We really are more than we think about ourselves. One Scripture even says we have become the righteousness of God in Christ! (2 Corinthians 5:21)

I dare you to believe these two radical truths:

1. What you do has no bearing on His love for you.
2. You are not what you do!! Your sins don't define you. You are actually a saint and not a sinner on the inside!

When we start knowing more of who we are, we are set free to live a different life in line with what He has done for us. And, by the way, it changes how you pray. You find yourself coming to the Lord saying, 'Here I am Father, the one You like. You like me because You are love, but I even dare to believe I'm likeable, 'cause I'm made in Your image and I'm clean before You!' This is the confidence the Bible talks about in approaching God (Hebrews 10:19). May *your* confidence in the radical love of the Father increase... and increase... and increase still more!!

Comfort

Let me be honest: I like comfort – warm fires, blankets, and lots of chocolate and ice creams. I've often heard preachers say, 'The problem with Christians in the West is that we are just too comfortable,' 'We are clinging to comfort which keeps us from clinging to God,' and other such things. Now I know what they mean. There is something about risk and adventure that grows our trust. I recently read a biography of St Francis of Assisi and his life could quite easily be described as austere by modern western standards, yet the faith God had given him was amazing. So for lots of reasons I do understand this perspective.

However, I do believe comfort is a gift of God. Obviously this can be material 'comfort' which is a good thing (not sure Francis of Assisi would have agreed!), but what I'm talking about is the comfort *God* loves to bring us. Paradoxically, one of the things we find hardest in our Christian lives is to allow ourselves to be comforted by God. Perhaps receiving comfort from Him feels like something appropriate for weaker Christians, younger believers and needy people, but for us, perhaps we feel the call is to be holy and strong men and women of God. When we imagine the apostle Paul, I expect the holy and strong man of God image comes to mind – stoned, shipwrecked, man of faith, etc... but how often do we remember that he also spoke of the 'Father of compassion and the God of all comfort, who comforts us in all our troubles, so that we can comfort those in any trouble with the comfort we ourselves have received from God' (2 Corinthians 1:3-4)?

Ok, so if 'big strong' Paul was saying this, what about big strong King David? Listen to Psalm 131:2: 'But I have stilled and quietened my soul; like a weaned child with its mother, like a weaned child is my soul within me.' Not exactly the mighty man image we often have of either of these guys. Yes they had strength within them, shown in some of what they endured, but it came from a place of comfort in the arms of a God who is the 'God of all comfort'. If we can just open our hearts and let Him hold us and love us, we will find a comfort flowing from His heart into our deepest wounds.

I love the fact that for a disobedient Israel the prophet receives the words:

Comfort, comfort my people, says your God. Speak tenderly to Jerusalem, and proclaim to her that her hard service has been completed, that her sin has been paid for.
Isaiah 40:1-2

Many of us have been so wounded by living in a broken world that we have, in order to survive, had to build up all sorts of defences within our souls to protect us from the searing, piercing reality of pain and remove ourselves from it. Often, even as Christians, a lot of our teaching acts to strengthen these defences, when it is focused around our faith and our works. But ultimately, pushing pain away doesn't work. This all causes us to live in a place distant from some of the most crucial aspects of the Father's heart: His gentleness, His tenderness, His softness, His affection and His comfort, and consequently a lot of our lives become like *'hard service'* (the result of the reality of sin): trying, pressing, pushing, proving, striving.

There is one answer: comfort. The comfort of the Father for our broken hearts. It's what makes us feel so safe around Him, to bear our wounds to Him over time, and have Him heal the depth of the pain in our hearts. We all need this comfort. There is something about an embrace that just speaks of comfort. When we feel someone is holding us and in no way telling us to 'pull ourselves together' or 'sort ourselves out', nor criticising us for our feelings – in that sort of safe embrace, our pain surfaces so much more easily. We can bear our wounds when we feel we are not rushed to show them and are held so unconditionally, knowing that what comes out of our hearts will be in no way criticised. This is how Father holds us.

. You may be thinking, 'This is all a bit sentimental, and I'm not sure what relevance it has to my Christian life.' Well, without this comforting aspect of His love, a lot of the brokenness in our souls stays there, not really leaving us free to grow into maturity. It's possible to have walked with the Lord for many years, grown in lots of ways, and perhaps even performed many miracles, yet still to have a deep need for this comfort. What I'm trying to say is that this comfort is what everybody needs, but for many of us, we've spent most of our lives detaching ourselves from acknowledging our need for it. Most of us find it easier to beat ourselves up: I'll never forget when I was at a Father-heart men's retreat in 2008, and in the middle of the talk the speaker said in front of all the others, 'Simon beats himself up, and I can understand it because I was like that.' I had hardly spoken to him that weekend, but he had obviously just seen it in me. So I understand if you find it hard to open up to God's comfort. So does God – He knows why it's so hard for you. He knows all your story.

But, you know the essence of Christianity is this loving, unconditional, all-accepting embrace of a Father so intent on healing you that He gave His only beloved Son to suffer Himself for all you have been through (whether as a result of things you have done or things done to you). What if we were to lay aside the religious way we can take the words of those preachers telling us to 'not be so comfortable' and instead believe the words of Isaiah that our 'hard service has been completed' and hear our Father saying, 'Comfort, comfort my people. Comfort to you little one.' Please stop being so hard on yourself; stop trying to hold it all together. He doesn't require it of you! Your hard service has been completed. Your sin has been paid for. He knows what you've been through. I don't think I've fully learnt yet not to beat myself up, but I do now know that He doesn't require it of me. He doesn't require it of any of us.

The comforting arms of the Father are around you all the time, unconditionally holding you no matter what... He holds you. Remember this next time you spend some time with Him. Whenever you sit with Him He embraces you. Whether you feel much or you feel little; whether you have a lot of faith or feel like you can hardly trust at all; if you are in a good place or a bad place; whether you are in sin or out of it... you are being held in the love of God. Nothing can separate you from His love (Romans 8:38-39).

'As a mother comforts her child, so will I comfort you' (Isaiah 66:13). Let Him comfort you in His arms.

Only Jesus can lead us to the Father

Jesus' ministry on earth was to show us what His Father is like and to make His Father known. His ministry in heaven is to bring us to His Father, by the Holy Spirit... There's a really great book out at the moment called *Heaven is for Real* which recounts a four-year-old's visit to heaven when he was critically ill in hospital. Out of the many conversations he had with his mum and dad in the following years, many chats he had had with Jesus in heaven came to light. One Good Friday, in talking about why Jesus died, Colton (aged about seven by now) said, 'Jesus told me He died on the cross so we could go see His Dad.'[18] It's the delight of our Lord and Saviour to lead us into the arms of His Father – He is the *way to the Father* (John 14:6)... It's what He came for.

We have often missed this central reality. But as glorious as our relationship with Jesus is, we can't fulfil our destiny as Christians by relating to Jesus alone, or even to Jesus and the Holy Spirit alone. Before you stone me as a heretic, let me say why I think this. In Romans, Paul says God predestined us 'to be conformed to the likeness of his Son' (Romans 8:29). If we are becoming like His Son, we can ask, 'Well, who/what is His Son?' Well, it's in the word – He's a 'Son'. How do you become like a Son? There's only one way – by having a Father... Jesus is our elder brother – listen to Hebrews where it talks about God bringing many 'sons to glory' (Hebrews 2:10). We are told, 'Jesus is not ashamed to call them brothers' (2:11). 'He says, "I will declare your name to my brothers"' (2:12). Whose name? Father's name.

Derek Prince, after 40 or so years of anointed ministry, prayer, fasting and casting out demons, came into an

---

[18] Todd Burpo with Lynn Vincent, *Heaven is for Real* (Nashville: Thomas Nelson, 2010), p111.

experience of God the Father's love for him in the final two years of his life. And he came to say of the verse, 'I am the way and the truth and the life. No one comes to the Father except through me' (John 14:6), that that verse speaks of a pathway and a destination, but that most of the church has got stuck on the way... Strangely we can sometimes feel that this is dishonouring to Jesus, but that's because we don't understand His own heart towards His Father. I heard a story of someone who was prayed for to experience the Father's love, but whenever he tried to see himself in the Father's arms, it was always Jesus' arms he saw himself in. Then one day he saw himself in the Father's arms, and the thing was, he saw Jesus at His right hand, looking so full of joy and essentially saying, 'Well done, you made it.' Jesus is our Lord, our Saviour, our Lover, our everything, and knowing the Father gives us an even deeper love for His Son, but we need to understand His heart to His Father in order to find our own place.

You see, Father wanted a family. Hebrews 2:11 says Jesus and we are 'of the same family'. Salvation was all about the Son seeing the love in the Father's heart for us who were made to be sons and daughters, seeing His brokenness at us being lost, and out of His great love for His Father saying, 'Father I'll go... I'll go to bring them back to you.'

Jesus is the only eternally begotten Son of God, to use theological talk. He is God and we are not; He is the second person of the Trinity and He has never fallen and never will. But we too are genuine sons and daughters of the same Father. We came from Him. That's why in other places Jesus is described as the 'firstborn' (Colossians 1:15; Romans 8:29; Hebrews 1:6) – this is not to suggest that He had a beginning, but to say that we were intended to be sons and daughters in His image.

So know this is what you were born to be – a son of the same Father as our Lord Jesus, loved by the same Father as our Lord

Jesus, loved with the same love. Does that sound too incredible? Listen to His prayer to His Father: 'You ... have loved them even as you have loved me' (John 17:23). Wow! That's a lot of love! That's all the love there is in the history of eternity... *all* coming to each of us at every moment! Perhaps if that truth hits our hearts it will finally help us relax in our Father's arms, rather than fear Him and run away covering ourselves with guilt, shame and fear.

Why am I saying this? Well, we sometimes have experiences where people who we look to, to show us the Father, let us down. In fact, anyone other than Jesus who we look to, to show us the Father, will in one way or another fail us simply because they can never represent the Father as He did – He was the only one to totally represent what He is like. I believe in spiritual fathers, mentors, leaders and authority, and I believe God wants us to be able to trust these people – however, if we 'put our trust' in these people, in one way or another we will end up disappointed. There has only ever been one who can lead us into Father's arms... Yes, men can point us in the right way, but only Jesus can lead us into that most intimate place.

So, if you have no one to show you the way, but you want to know your Father in heaven more; if you want to experience being fathered and loved by a Father, just pray a simple prayer: 'Jesus take me to the Father;' 'Jesus lead me into Father's arms.'

He knows the way, it's where He came from... John 1:18 says, 'No one has ever seen God, but God the one and only, who is at the Father's side [literally 'in the Father's bosom'] has made him known.' Then this theme is followed all the way through John's gospel until 20:17 where Jesus says to Mary after He has risen, 'I am returning to my Father and your Father, to my God and your God.' Just read through John 14–17 if you want to get a sense of the relationship Jesus had and has with the Father, which He came to lead us back to. He finished His prayer by saying to His Father, 'I have made you known to them, and will continue to make you known in order that the love you have for me may be in them and that I myself may be in them' (John 17:26). He says, '*I will continue to make you known to them...*'

This ministry carries on today, and it has been my experience of relating to Jesus, that it is very close to His heart.

In 2007, the Lord told me to write as if I was having a vision of Jesus. As I wrote I found I received very clear pictures of what I was writing about. Throughout the vision, Jesus would take me to places and talk to me about His Father. Then, in the final part of the vision, He actually took me up a mountain to meet His Father... and as we were coming towards the Father, the Father was running towards us with open arms. That is my home; that is your home; that is Jesus' home! We really have been given more than we realise! He leads us there to stay in direct communion with the Father. As He said to the disciples, 'I am not saying that I will ask the Father on your behalf. No, the Father himself loves you' (John 16:26-27). Why not camp out with those words? THE FATHER HIMSELF LOVES YOU! HE IS YOUR HOME!

Accepting process

Most real coffee lovers pull a slightly funny face if you offer them instant coffee – have you noticed? Actually, I don't mind instant coffee, but it's interesting, isn't it? We live in a world where everything is instant. Instant coffee, instant custard, instant credit, instant access to any website anywhere in the world... and if our computer connection is slow and it takes two minutes to load something, we start getting annoyed with the computer!! But things that are instant rarely taste as good! How often we want to be instant with our walk with the Lord. We see our own problems and what needs changing, and we want Father to sort it all out in a moment – or even worse, we expect ourselves to sort it all out in an instant.

Now I don't want to devalue 'instant' things in Christianity... I mean, God can do in a day what we would expect to take a lifetime, or longer: in three hours on the cross, Jesus transformed the whole of history. When you and I came to Him we received His forgiveness of our sins, past, present and future – we were given a new heart, and moved out from being under the kingdom of darkness into the kingdom of light, seated in the heavenly places in Christ. Now that is a lot of instant change! Much more miraculous and a lot nicer tasting than instant coffee!

However, I think where a lot of us get confused and discouraged is we think that because God can act instantly and has done in the past, we shouldn't have things in our lives that still need healing and changing. Have you ever cried out to God about a response you don't understand in yourself, a hurt you feel, or an issue you face and said, 'I've been struggling with this for so long. Why haven't You changed it; why don't You?' I have... but as I have journeyed with the Father, I have begun to see the importance of accepting 'process' in my relationship with Him. I have also seen how hard I find that, and asked Him to help me. So let me share some of what I have discovered so far.

God made a world with seasons and with night and day, with time which progresses, and with gradual change over time. I guess before the Fall seasons would have looked different, but I'm pretty sure they would have still existed, so this tells me process is in the heart of God. Solveig, who I mentioned earlier, has released a CD called *Seasons of the soul* and it brilliantly has a song for every month in the year and an accompanying line or two of poetry tracking the progress of the soul within the changing of seasons... Seasons are about process![19]

Every six months I try to take a week away with God. This last time I was in the Brecon Beacons and God spoke to my heart about process through the creation around me. Often if I'm needing to hear God on a retreat, I look for something in creation like a stream or a flower that my heart is drawn to and then ask what God could be saying about my life through this. This time, though, I didn't need to look. In front of my window was a tree that had started turning to beautiful autumn colours, except that only a quarter of it had turned to these colours – the rest was still green. Now I love the autumn, and had stayed at the same place in the height of autumn four years before and the place had been alight with the bright yellows, hazel oranges and deep reds of autumn... This time this tree and most others were only partially turned, and I began longing for the ability to click my fingers and bring on the fullness of autumn there and then. Of course, I couldn't do that, and I can't do that with my own life either. As with the seasons, all I can do is wait and accept the gentle, at times 'slow', and often even unseen, work of God through which change occurs. There are dramatic

---

[19] You can get this online through Amazon, Cross Rhythms, or her own website http://ssnygaard.com/appletree/ (accessed 23rd April 2014).

moments in nature – a sudden budding, a gale which blows things around, a bird of prey swooping in a moment to catch its prey – but often the change of seasons occurs as a gradual change which cannot even be noticed at the time, but only as one looks back at how things were.

What I needed to see was that if I didn't accept the tree as it was, without full transformation, I would not enjoy the beauty that was all around... The same is true with my journey with God and yours. It's so easy to miss the beauty of where we are now in our journeys, simply because we are not satisfied that everything is not yet fully sorted. But you see, we are changing all the time.

What stunts joy in most of our lives is that we often can't accept ourselves until everything is sorted out and how we want it, and we can find it hard to accept that God doesn't act as we would. However, He loves us at every stage of our journeys! You see, love does not demand, expect or even ask change of us. He loves us as we are at every moment, whatever still needs changing, and in accepting us, by the very fact of being accepted completely, that love changes us. He doesn't see you as more beautiful when you are more healed than you were before. He came to you and accepted you as you were before anything in your life had been changed (Romans 5:8-10). He SO SOooo LOVES you! He loves the spring, summer and autumn of your life, and all the in-betweens.[20] He is in no rush... He is happy with you now!

But where there are difficult things we are waiting on God to heal or help us with, it can be so easy to lose heart. I can't offer you easy answers – there are none – but I can point you to the nature of love. You see, God is gentle. In your life, He has been,

---

[20] My friend Sue was once having a conversation with the Lord about the different seasons of her life. She got to autumn and she asked Him, 'What about winter, Lord?' She felt Him say that there isn't winter in His kingdom.

at every moment, even in the hardest times, gently working around some of your deepest wounds, removing one root after another, until He can get right to the tap root of the particular issue which is causing you difficulty... He does this in a way which doesn't force you, in a way that acknowledges your free will as a human being and allows you to let go of things in your own time. I know this can be hard to see, but it really is His wisdom that He doesn't do it all in one go. I'm not sure we could take it if He did. Instead, He gently works, little by little, until we are ready to receive miraculous change. But so often it is a hidden work. As with the seasons, we often look back and see how far we've come, but only over a process, and in time. When you see the issue in front of you, sometimes that can be all you see, but God is working for your total freedom! Trust, beloved of God! Spring never fails to travel its way through summer to autumn! It will be the same with your life. It will! You will see! Let's be clear – God did not plan or cause the things that have been hard in our lives. They were never His plan. He is the one healing us, and He is doing it over time because it's the best way possible.

I heard a talk recently by Mark Gyde, who founded a ministry called 'A Father to you', and he said that he had been in the car asking the Lord the same question. Having seen the pain in the people he was ministering to, he said, 'Father, why don't you just click your fingers and make everything ok?'

He felt the Father respond, saying, 'What do you think it would be like if I did?'

Then from his heart came the response, 'It would be clinical and robotic.'

The Father then said to him, 'If I did, you would not seek me with your hearts,' and he began to see that there is a *beauty in process*.[21]

---

[21] http://www.fatherheart.tv/webcast-audio-archives/ 'The Beauty of Process' (Mark Gyde – 25thApril 2012).

The seasons show me this is true. As I began to accept the beauty around me *as it was* that week on retreat, I began to experience the beauty of it all in such deep ways. Perhaps if we can start to accept ourselves as we are now, not demanding change of ourselves or God on our schedule, but waiting in expectant hope, then there will be a joy in our lives that we have not known before. Life-changing sudden healings, revelations and encounters will come, and, beloved, rejoice when they do... but let Father also open your eyes to the deep, unseen, gentle work of His hand in your heart at every moment of your life!

My wife was honest enough to tell me when I read this to her that it didn't answer all her questions on this issue! I expect it doesn't answer all yours either – but I hope it encourages your heart that it's ok to be on a journey, and not have everything sorted. Love is coming to you now like the sun, wind and rain come to the earth and bring the amazing change from one season to another. Love is coming to you now and breathing beauty into your life. Love will do everything that needs to be done – all you have to do is let that love come and not try and bring about the change in your own strength. Blessings upon you! Enjoy the beautiful process!!

Make every effort to enter His rest

Busy, busy, busy... 'I'm busy, busy, busy;' 'I'm just so busy at the moment;' 'My diary is so full;' 'I wish I could stop, just for a moment;' 'If only... but I can't. I have no choice but to be busy, busy, busy.' Sound familiar? Hear it in conversations? Hear it in your own heart? Work, home, friends, hobbies, diaries. Do... do... or as one speaker put it, 'There's a lot of doodoo around!'[22] We genuinely believe we are stuck and have no choice. We have a moment of longing for something different, and then return to our busyness. Here's a question for you: 'Is it true that we have no choice?' Ponder it for a moment... Do you have no choice, but to be very busy?

As you ponder, consider these words from Henri Nouwen, someone who grappled his whole life with this struggle within himself. I like where he came to:

It's true that a lot of people say 'I wish I had some more time. I wish I could be more alone'.... It is a very mixed complaint, because their busyness is self-created. If you are critical about why you are so busy, you will quickly find out that you don't have to be. There is absolutely no reason for most people to be as busy as they are. You want to earn more money than you need. You want to see more television than you need. You want to read more books than you need to read. You want to see more people. You want to keep in touch with too many friends. You want to travel too much. You can even be busy with looking for the meaning of solitude! ... If you help a person who is busy and who complains that there's not enough solitude, that basically is a call for radical conversion. Here we go to the depths of it; it is a question of spiritual identity. If you are busy, very

---

[22] In a talk by Peter Jackson.

busy, ask yourself 'why am I so busy?' Perhaps you want to prove something.[23]

Henri also said that people either define themselves by 'what they do', 'what people say about them', or 'what they have', and that any of those three leads to a wrong view of ourselves and could also lead to a busyness that we believe we have no control over. He shows how each of Jesus' temptations was to believe these three different lies about who He was, but that His response was to say, 'No, I am not these things; I am the beloved of God.' You too are the beloved. As Henri says to us, 'Don't go running round, don't start to prove to everybody that you're beloved. "You already are beloved." That is what God says to us.'[24]

I chose Henri on this topic because I remember eight years ago reading something wise and simple that he wrote which changed my approach to rest time, solitude and time with God. He simply said:

We may have to write it in black and white on our daily calendar so that nobody else can take away this period of time. Then we will be able to say to our friends, neighbours, students, customers, clients, or patients, 'I'm sorry, but I've already made an appointment at that time and it can't be changed.'[25]

This was one of those pieces of advice that you never forget! That year I started taking a day a week just to be with God, but I found that although I organised my work around that easily

---

[23] Henri Nouwen, in conversation with Philip Roderick, *Beloved* (Norfolk: Canterbury Press, 2007), p10-12.
[24] Henri Nouwen, in conversation with Philip Roderick, *Beloved*, p13.
[25] Henri J. M. Nouwen, *The Only Necessary Thing*, compiled and edited by Wendy Wilson Greer (London: Darton, Longman and Todd Ltd, 2000), p46.

enough, my friends and my phone also wanted that time. I also faced a lot of self-doubt – 'Is it ok for me to spend time like this?' 'Is it selfish?' 'Is it lazy?' 'Will it do me harm?' But Henri's words, and the Spirit of God, sustained me that year, so that I didn't give up. And about a year later, I met a hermit in the Shetland Isles, and as I sat having coffee with him it was as if the Lord was speaking directly to me saying, 'Simon, I know who you are. You are a different shape to many people, but I want to show you how I have made you to be.' From that time on I started exploring retreats and going away for periods of time. But everyone is different, and what everyone needs is individual to them.

There are people who are more 'active' in their calling and those who are more 'contemplative', but everyone needs rest to be at peace. Throughout the history of the church it has been seen that there is a call for some to an 'active' life and some to a 'contemplative' life. Today it is hardly recognised that a contemplative life could be an option. But no matter what your calling, we all need something of the contemplative within us.

What is 'the contemplative'? It is about being fully present to God, an ability to rest and enjoy nature, stillness in the now, and enjoying love for the sake of love. Do you realise that God loves to be present in the moment with us, and He loves us to be present with Him.

As a picture of this I love the story of Mary and Martha. Of Mary we hear, '[Martha] had a sister called Mary, who sat at the Lord's feet listening to what he said' (Luke 10:39). I love it that she sat... and listened so much that she was absorbed in the moment, enough to not worry about what needed doing around her. She had put the 'to do' list aside, and unlike many of us she hadn't waited until she got to the end of it!! Mostly in society we tend to look down on people like this as lazy or unaware, and we tend to see ourselves in this way if we spend too long as Mary. The natural question came from Martha:

'Lord, don't you care that my sister has left me to do the work by myself?' (Luke 10:40), a question a lot of us might have asked in the same situation. Jesus surprises us with His answer. Instead of saying, 'Yes Mary, you really need to be a bit more responsible about your spiritual life, there are things to be done, after all,' He says, 'Martha, Martha ... you are worried and upset about many things, but only one thing is needed. Mary has chosen what is better, and it will not be taken away from her' (Luke 10:41-42).

Perhaps when we feel that sense of guilt about resting, we could take that phrase from Jesus: *'only one thing is needed'*, and let it feed our hearts.

Now I'm not criticising activity. Activity is good. God is in activity as well as in rest, and I have many friends who can work very hard and yet keep a sense of God's rest within it... But for all of us, *we need to be ok with resting*. It's in the heart of God. If you don't believe me, look at the first thing Adam knew of God his Father in the garden. He knew him as a God of rest who had completed His work of creation. Sabbath is a key theme in the Old Testament, which is then completed in Hebrews, where it talks about a 24-7 Sabbath rest for the people of God – in other words, a rest we can live out of all the time. So first and foremost rest is an attribute of the heart, where we know that we are loved and accepted as we are. This brings a tremendous self-acceptance and rest. But along with this, it's pretty hard to rest without actually taking time in the practical: i.e. – STOPPING!! The writer to the Hebrews must have had a smile on his face when he said, 'Let us, therefore, make every effort to enter that rest' (Hebrews 4:11). 'Effort' and 'rest' seem opposed, but I think what he saw was that so much in the world around us, in the church, and the brokenness within our own hearts, wars against rest, so that it takes something radical and courageous to stand up for a different way.

Our culture surrounds us with busyness and the lie that constant activity is the only way, but I want to ask, 'Why? Why does it have to be like this?' Are we not being constantly kept from a freedom of heart and mind to rest because of what our society tells us? As the writer to the Hebrews says, 'Anyone who enters God's rest also rests from his own work, just as God did from his' (Hebrews 4:10). This doesn't mean that we will never do anything; it just takes away the sense of having to do anything. That's the starting point. Jesus has done all that needs to be done. Father wants us to live from our hearts – and that is not about living from 'have-tos'.

Why do we find it hard to embrace what Mary embraced? Perhaps it's that sense of obligation. But perhaps it's also the fear-based feeling of 'if we don't do it – who is going to?' Barry Adams, who wrote the 'Father's love letter',[26] was asking the Lord about this passage one time, not understanding how things would get done if there weren't Marthas around, and the Lord said to him, 'Remember the feeding of the 5,000. Perhaps I would have done the same.'[27] Challenging thought, isn't it? Ultimately, we are dependent on God for our provision.

So if you need times just to be, just to rest with your loving Father... well, retreats are certainly one way you can rest in God's heart full of love, but He is everywhere and wanting to pour His love upon you wherever you are and give you rest. The key is your heart. Stop to think about it. Do you really think that God is like that, the way that we are with ourselves? Do you really think He doesn't allow us a moment's rest?

Why not ask Him to show you?

YOU ARE THE BELOVED.
You are free.
You get to choose how busy you are!

---

[26] http://www.fathersloveletter.com/ (accessed 19th June 2014).
[27] Heard in a talk by Barry Adams.

If you want to, you could start today to 'make every effort to enter that rest'!

Perhaps it would help to see the affectionate smile not only on the face of the writer to the Hebrews, but also on the Father's face who spoke these words through him. Really these words are words of great love. They are words telling you that you are loved enough to be allowed to rest. And in this rest you will be awakened, over time, to a Father who has been loving you every moment of your life. He is loving you now! Rest in His love, beloved child.

God doesn't have two sides

It's interesting to me that for most of us when we start thinking or having revelation about the holiness of God, our first reaction is to recoil in thinking of our own sinfulness. Isaiah cried, 'Woe to me ... For I am a man of unclean lips' (Isaiah 6:5). Peter said to Jesus, 'Go away from me, Lord; I am a sinful man' (Luke 5:8). A member of the Urban Retreat was sharing with me recently that she had been watching a scientific programme about the universe which made her feel overwhelmed by the bigness of God, and she thought, 'How can I even come near to you, Lord?' But just as she thought this a picture flashed through her mind of a father picking up a little child. This gave her peace. There is no doubt about it – we are very little and He is very big! But if we look at His holiness as an abstract concept with Him up there and us down here, we will come to a very misguided conclusion. We need to look closer, right into His heart. Who is He, the one who made us? Is He just God up there, or is He our Father in His truest nature who made us and loves us?

You see, I have felt for a long time that, in the church, there exists a separation between the holiness and the love of God. Some of this comes from teaching we have had, but more than this, it is the effects of the Fall within humanity which tend to separate everything: love and holiness, mind and heart, man and woman, father and son, and more. John said very clearly, 'God is love' (1 John 4:16). I believe that he meant something more than to name one of the many of God's attributes. I believe that he was boldly telling us that you will not find anything in the nature of God outside of LOVE. I don't wish to criticise what anyone believes, or start a theological argument, but it seems clear to me that in a lot of the church, present and past, we have lived with a belief that God has two sides – a loving side and a holy side. Because of His holy side He has to treat us in a certain way because of our sin, otherwise known as punishment, and we tend to refer to this as His justice, but because He is also loving, He doesn't want us to have to die and so He punishes Jesus instead, and we then get to go free. The good part of this is we know there is no punishment because Jesus has taken it. The problem is that it leaves us with a very deep insecurity about the nature of the God we are meant to be able to call a loving Father, as we don't see how we can really know He doesn't still want to punish us, and therefore how we can really feel safe with Him.

I've done everything to avoid reading too much theology since I finished Bible college 11 years ago in 2003! However, I did recently hear something from an American theologian which I thought was absolutely profound, so I'm going to share it. He said that if you look at the early church, the apostles and some of the key Early Church Fathers such as Irenaeus and Athanasius, you can see that the heart of their understanding of God's holiness was that He was three persons in intimate relationship. This came from them seeing that Jesus was clearly related to a Father who loved Him and gave the Holy Spirit. Instead of one solitary person up there far away and all of us down here, God was a dance of love into which He included us in creation and redemption. He pointed out that where it went a bit wrong was with Augustine who said many wonderful things, but because of influences from Greek philosophy, believed that there was, as well as the Trinity, this other essence of the pure holiness of God which still leaves us with the feeling of being separated from Him. This theologian wanted to suggest that if we could drill down into the very core of who God is we would find *relationship* – a relationship of perfect love.

It is this love with which the Father loves the Son and the Son loves the Father in the Spirit, that caused the Son to say,

'I'll go Papa, send me,'[28] and the Father paid the ultimate cost of watching the one He loved die... for us. So this really is His holiness – that He is pure love. What does holiness mean? To be set apart, to be above, to be other. His ways are higher than ours; His thoughts higher than ours (Isaiah 55:9). But what is so clearly different and set apart about our Father? It is that He is pure, undiluted, holy, gentle, passionate and blazing love...

Remember, 'God is love' (1 John 4:8, 16).[29]

This is what the angels worship Him for, and why the elders bow down. They see One who is so loving in His nature that the greatest expression of that love is that He would allow His beloved Son to come and die on our behalf. He is HOLY LOVE and He is LOVING HOLINESS, but His love and His holiness are not separate. You don't have to look for His loving side, whilst fearing that He has another scary holy side. There is nothing scary about God. Even the fear of the Lord in Scripture is connected to His love. Listen to the psalmist: 'But with you there is forgiveness; therefore you are feared' (Psalm 130:4). Allow me to paraphrase: 'I can't believe how loving you are, how good; therefore we stand in awe of you.' And His justice, to me, is not about Him having to punish sin, but that He fights on our side, for us. 'God presented Him as a sacrifice of atonement ... He did this to demonstrate his justice' (Romans 3:25). I do not believe that there is a shred of punishment in His nature. He disciplines us, we know this, but this, though it can be hard, is to heal and help us. Even His anger is an expression of His love – He hates to see us suffer. Even hell is an expression of love – He gives people a great gift of being able to reject Him if they so choose: free will. The fact that some do breaks His heart, but love can never force.

I had a moment similar to our retreat member's moment that I shared at the beginning. One night, when I was in Wales a few

---

[28] Words echoed by the prophet Isaiah (Isaiah 6:8).
[29] Italics added.

months ago, I could see the stars clearly, so I lay down on the grass, looking at them, awed. I started to think how awesome God was, how He was totally beyond anything I could think about or imagine... but as I started to think this, and sensed a similar temptation to go down the 'woe is me' avenue, something occurred to me. Scripture says I am made in the image of God, in His likeness (Genesis 1:26-27). If He is that amazing and He is my true Father and He says I am like Him, I must be a lot more than I see about myself! Dutch Sheets, who has written books on intercessory prayer, points out that if you had seen Adam, God's son, in the Garden of Eden, you would probably have gone – 'Wow, for a minute there I thought that was God!'[30] Precious son, precious daughter – you are made in the image of the Holy One; you are His very own; you do not need to fear Him. Yes He is awesome, yes He is way beyond all we can imagine, yes there is a mystery to Him – the more I journey the more I see the mystery... He is the Lion and the Lamb, there is a strength to His character, and there is a deep tenderness, but all this is His LOVE.

In Colossians, Paul says that love is the reality that binds all other virtues together in perfect unity (Colossians 3:14). If we take this and apply it to the nature of God, it is love that describes His core, or even His 'limits', as one anonymous Carthusian writer puts it.[31] We need to understand all that we know about Him within the context of love and see nothing outside of love. We need to see all His feelings in Scripture, all His attributes and all His actions in the context of this love, each of them a different expression of love. Beloved, your Father does not have another side to Him – He loves you because He is love and only love. I'm well aware that we all get this to only one degree or another. I've believed it for ten years

---

[30] Dutch Sheets, *Intercessory Prayer* (California: Regal, 1996), p26.
[31] A Carthusian, *They Speak by Silences* (Herefordshire: Gracewing Publishing, 2006), p51.

and experienced it in many ways, but I find much in my heart that is still afraid that I could be wrong... you probably do too. Still, I'm committed to the journey of discovering that I really can be carefree and love life, knowing that there is One who will always be on my side (Romans 8:31) and who, whilst He has many varied characteristics, has only one side: LOVE.

'You can't make sense of this... It's nonsense!'

Do you ever find yourself trying to work God out? My advice after 17 years of knowing the Lord is simple – don't bother! Knowledge was never meant to rule our lives. If we just look around us we see that knowledge seems to rule our world. So much is geared around knowing more, so that we can achieve more. But remember Adam and Eve? Two trees. One of life, of union, of living out of relationship, of love... of *knowing*. This is what we were made for. And of course, there was the other tree, the one they ate from – the 'tree of the *knowledge* of good and evil' (Genesis 2:9, 17). Not just the tree *of* good and evil, but 'of the *knowledge of* good and evil'.

Now your mind is an amazing tool, but that's what it is – a tool – it's not YOU. Your heart is you... your mind is yours. It's not you and it's certainly not God – an awful lot of our problems in and outside the church come from having made the mind god (what I mean by this is that we have exalted the mind above the role God created it to play, so that what we can trust and believe is often determined by whether it is reasonable or not). By 'heart', I don't mean your emotions. I mean the core of your personality, who you truly are. Now of course it's not just that our philosophies have exalted the mind's role. It's also that we have lived in a painful world, and for a lot of God's children it has been safer to live from the mind rather than from the heart. Many people have done everything they can to close themselves off from their hearts.

I think for much of the earlier part of my life, knowledge was a safer place to be – God has had to undo this in me over a period of time. A year and a bit into Bible college I was trying to work out everything about God through human reasoning. The first thing, I remember, that began to undo this tendency in me was going to a conference where an Argentinean revivalist was speaking. As he was speaking, I found myself arguing with my mind, with everything he was saying, until suddenly it was as if my eyes were opened, and beyond any process of reasoning with my brain, I could tell for certain that most of what he was saying was correct. I started to see that there is a deeper *knowing* than knowledge.

All the deepest spiritual experiences are like this, you know. They actually bypass our minds.[32] With our minds we may reflect on them or 'explain' them to others, but we do not get closer to God through our minds... through knowledge. Why? Because it was never meant to be the way. The only reason people struggle to see this is that the effects of the Fall have turned the world inside out. Most people think that to experience God, you need to put a thought in your mind and think about it and then try and get this truth down into your heart, but we were created to relate to God with our heart directly touching His, and our mind, will and emotions experiencing the effects of that, and our bodies also. Think of a romantic relationship: to get closer to the one you love, you don't read their autobiography and study it (if they are lucky enough to have one). No. You move your heart towards theirs!

The Lord had to do this in layers with me – so six years after the experience I described, I was away on a Father-heart retreat in the Yorkshire Dales, which was all about receiving God's love. We were praying to hand the keys of our lives over to Father and give Him control. When they came to pray for me, a guy called Jim piped up and said, 'You need to let go of your mind, Simon. *You can't make sense of this... It's NONSENSE!'* The moment he said 'nonsense', the joy of the Lord filled me and I

---

[32] This may sound like a strong thing to say, but what I am saying is that God created us to live heart to heart with Him from the inside out, but the result of the Fall is that the world is living from the outside in! I am saying here that love bypasses our minds, that it's not reasonable... if we can let go of the belief that love has to go through the filter of our minds first, we may start to be able to experience it.

laughed a deep belly laugh. All my life I had tried to make sense of God, and here on a weekend about receiving His love, somewhere deep down I thought that if I could just make sense of it, then I would be able to receive it... and here was the Lord clearly saying to me that it's nonsense. NON SENSE – in other words, you cannot fit the things of God through the filter of your mind. I realised at that point why that unknown medieval Mystic wrote *The Cloud of Unknowing*. We come close to God not through what we can know, but in our hearts.

In recent years, as I have seen the value of silence – just sitting with God, many times where I am not saying any words and He is not saying any either – I have seen this even more, that the love of God is beyond what the mind can grasp. In the silence, He has taken this revelation deeper. At times I've battled with the silence and it has often made little sense to my mind. About a year ago I was battling with it, sitting alone in the prayer hut that we have in the Urban Retreat garden, when something struck me from deep down: 'you can't fit God into your head'. He is too big and our heads are too small to fit him! That's the point. I came and shared this with my friend Solveig, who was sitting inside in the Retreat, and I think it amused her. Shortly after, I went on a week's retreat in beautiful Wales. As God met me in the silence, His silence, the verse that was so strong to me at that time was 'Trust in the Lord with all your heart and lean not on your own understanding' (Proverbs 3:5). And I saw that *trust* is something we can only do with our hearts! To the extent we trust, we will feel safe to live out of our hearts; to the extent we don't, we will most likely try to work God out with our minds... But let me save you the effort: don't bother – it will only exhaust you!

Instead, come close to Him in your heart, to that place of deep communion with Father, Son and Spirit, that you were created to live out of – there He is; there He dwells. Experiencing the love of God is not something you have the ability to process! To receive it, somehow you need to open your heart and let it be poured in. Love is not some philosophy, or choice – a mere act of the will. Love is reality... love is 'stuff', and it can only be experienced in your heart. He is loving *you* right now. *Your* Daddy, *your* Papa, who loves you with everything He has. He is jumping for joy over you (Zephaniah 3:17). Perhaps, like me, the only way to open your heart more to this reality could be to hear the words, 'You can't make sense of this – it's nonsense.' Just receive. Let yourself be loved!

Pick up thy plastic hammer!

My friend Robert tells this wonderful story of building the Christian bed and breakfast that he has been running. He tells of how his young grandson Daniel was on the building site one day as he was looking after him. Daniel wanted to join in... so Daniel was given his toy plastic hammer to join in with the work! At the end of the day, when the work was accomplished, Daniel said, 'Didn't we do well, Granddad?! I did that whole window by myself.' Robert's point was this: did Daniel help one bit with getting the building work done? No! Did he make it a lot more fun by being there? Yes!

This is so like us with the Lord. When God starts using us, we get all these big ideas that we are changing the world, and that God would be struggling without us. We even develop theologies to go with it of how God's work in the world depends on us, our action, our choices, our prayer, our faith... and all the while our Father is just smiling and saying, 'It's really great fun to have you around.' Co-workers? Yes, but our part in the deal is to be the little children with our plastic hammers. Please don't get me wrong; I'm not downplaying our value. What was Daniel's value in Robert's eyes? Infinite. It's the same with us and the Father – but it's really not us doing the work!

This really does take the pressure off. Instead of asking Father to come and join with our projects and our ministries and our works and bless them (which He will do), our focus is to look for what He is doing and to join in.

Jesus said to become like little children (Matthew 18:3; 19:14; Mark 10:14-16). I think so much of our focus in our Christian communities is to grow up, become mature, and be able to do the things of the kingdom. We take the way the natural works where we become more and more independent of our parents and apply it to the spiritual – but Jesus said to become like little children! In the natural, it is healthy that I don't depend on my earthly parents for resources. In the spiritual, the more dependent I am, the more I grow! Jesus was God incarnate, yet He said, 'The Son can do nothing by himself' (John 5:19). I kind of think if it's good enough for Jesus, it's good enough for me. This life is really good fun! Papa can do absolutely anything!

In my spiritual journey, I have known this for quite a while, yet the Lord recently reminded me of this truth. It seems to be quite easy to start living from self-effort rather than depending on the Father, and not realise you are doing it.

One day God spoke to Jack Winter and said, 'Rather than a big boy with a little Father, be a little boy with a big Father.'[33]

This is a place where we know we're dependent on Him for our core need – to be LOVED. We're dependent on Him to bring any blessing on those around us. We are COMPLETELY dependent on Him!!

The truth is, 'a little child' is what you are, whether you are 9 or 90. This really isn't degrading or offensive. Your Father has been around a long time... you can never be older than Him! Your heart can be free if you can know this truth.

'Humble yourself' (Matthew 18:4; 1 Peter 5:6; James 4:10). Let yourself be held and carried. He is changing the world! He doesn't need you to do it... but He loves having you around!

Father, open our eyes to see that we can let You have control... You really are able to handle it! We know we keep trying to do it in our own strength. Thank You that You smile, and enjoy having us by Your side! You really are a wonderful Father.

---

[33] Jack Winter, *The Homecoming* (Seattle: Ywam Publishing, 1997), p20.

Learning from the Desert Fathers: the power of silence

In the fourth and fifth centuries AD, when the church was becoming more institutional (around the time of Constantine and beyond), individuals, led by the Holy Spirit, started finding their way out into the Egyptian desert to seek God in silence and solitude. Over time, these hermits formed communities of solitaries in the desert. We have a collection of their sayings and know a little about their lives. It seems that people would go out to the desert to consult them and ask for wisdom.

They found that not just solitude was needed, but also silence, in order to encounter the depths of God. As they sought God in this way they found that battles opened up within them – temptations and struggles – but they also found a peace that was deeper than all these things. The silence seemed to be a way to come closer to God, but was also a reality of the presence of God that was able to be given away. Here's just a little quote to give a flavour of what they lived in:

> Archbishop Theophilus came to the desert to visit Abba Pambo [one of the Desert Fathers]. But Abba Pambo did not speak to him. When the brethren finally said to Pambo, 'Father, say something to the archbishop, so that he may be edified', he replied: 'If he is not edified by my silence, he will not be edified by my speech'.[34]

Our world teaches us to run from silence and fill our lives with noise and words... to the extent that most people live in fear of silence. But, if God is a God of love, what have we to

---

[34] Henri Nouwen, *The Way of the Heart: the Spirituality of the Desert Fathers and Mothers* (New York: Harper One, an imprint of Harper Collins Publishers, 1991), p44.

fear when all is silent? Yes, we may encounter more fully our own inner struggles, but in that place we find the depths of the love and grace of God, so that out of that silence we can live out of a deeper peace than it is possible to otherwise. I recommend having space in your days, weeks and years simply to be silent before God, perhaps even to go on a silent retreat somewhere.

Antony, one of the first and most well known of the Desert Fathers, went to the desert for 20 years, before returning to have a ministry amongst people. In the desert he experienced difficulties and battles, but he also came to a peace in the love of Jesus that was deeper than all these. As Henri Nouwen says, when Anthony left the desert:

> He took his solitude with him and shared it with all who came to him. Those who saw him described him as balanced, gentle and caring. He had become so Christlike, so radiant with God's love, that his entire being was ministry.[35]

I love all the stuff today that's being spoken about breaking down the sacred and secular divide, seeing that all creation belongs to God, and that He wants to transform society from within. However, if we think that society can be fully transformed from within without us ever taking leave of it in one way or another, I think we will find it won't work. Jesus often withdrew to solitary places – He spent 40 days in the desert at one point. Paul had years in the desert before his ministry started. There are so many mindsets, so many ways of being and doing around us that don't really come out of the depths of the love of God – therefore, to really live from those depths, even if we're not called to flee to the desert, we need some sort of nearby desert to flee to, whether it's our room, a retreat or elsewhere. The much neglected ancient paths of

---

[35] Henri Nouwen, *The Way of the Heart: the Spirituality of the Desert Fathers and Mothers*, p32.

solitude, silence and stillness are a vital part of learning to live continually in the love of God – this will look different for each person according to their shape, character and calling, but I suggest that everyone needs degrees of solitude, silence and stillness in their lives.

Silence leads us into the mystery of the love of God who is beyond all our thoughts and words. The mystery is in Christ, who showed us that His Father is our Father, and that He loves us as we are. This mystery cannot be captured by any individual word or thought about it. Sometimes, the best thing can be to sit in silence, allow our thoughts to be still, and rest in the mystery of love.

If you feel inspired by the Desert Fathers, it may help you to read a little more about them. Just remember when reading about them that there were ascetic extremes amongst their lives and teachings, and sometimes an overly negative view of the body, but this does not take away from the fact that these men really came to understand the world of the heart.

Learning from the Celtic Christians: the joy of journeying

The beginnings of Christianity in the British Isles have a richness and depth to them. The freedom and creativity of Celtic culture lent itself easily to an expression of the faith that was itself free and led by the Holy Spirit. I love that for the Celtic Christians the wild goose was a symbol for the Holy Spirit, in that He was untamed and free!

I won't bore you with too much history, but in a very simplified way of saying it: Patrick took the faith to Ireland and it spread dramatically, with Ireland becoming a centre of Celtic monasticism and mission in the fifth century AD. Columba then took a journey from there over the water to Scotland and formed a community of prayer and mission on the small island of Iona in the sixth century. Aidan then journeyed from there, in the seventh century, over to Lindisfarne, an island off the north coast of England. From here many journeyed down into the rest of England and on into Europe with a freedom of heart and message.

The Celtic Christians were also influenced by the Desert Fathers, whom I wrote about previously, and so the values of silence, stillness and solitude were important to them. With these I would say that the Celtic Christians also carried as important a focus on creation, creativity and community. However, for me, the value that stands out is their focus on *journeying* in all of these things, both in terms of actual journeys taken at the leading of the Spirit,[36] and in terms of seeing the whole of life as a journey.

Patrick went back to Ireland, originally the land of his slavery, in response to a dream where the Irish were calling to

---

[36] A good example would be 'Brendan's Voyage'. This was a journey on the sea embarked upon at the Spirit's leading.

him. A journey – NO PLAN – and look at where it led him. Columba set sail from Ireland – NO PLAN – and look at where it led him. He didn't even know he would end up in Iona!! Aidan went to Lindisfarne in response to an invitation from the king of the area, but still with no real plan by today's way of living, and that island has been a blessing to so many...

I went to that island recently for a retreat, not really knowing why I was going. I normally like to go to places where I know I can be alone in a safe and peaceful setting. This time, though, I just sensed a need in me to journey and explore. I found that God ministered to me in the manor hotel, looking out to sea over a Mars bar and cola, and through chatting to the shopkeeper in the local store, as well as in the solitude of my room. The Celtic Christians remind us that God's presence fills the whole of creation, and of the beauty of coming in an attitude of peace to every person we meet along the way.

Our world has become so full of plans, meetings, agendas... that we feel everything has to be prepared. We believe we need to have a plan for where our lives are heading. Let me ask you a countercultural question: 'Why?' I think if we answer this question honestly, then we may find that some of our answers are not based entirely on faith. Do we always need to know the way we're heading when we start off on a journey? Can it not be exciting to follow the lead of our heart in a certain direction, leaving the outcome in the hands of our loving Father?

I love this quote from Karen Lowe:

The 'Peregrinatio' of the Celtic monks has been challenged from a modernist mindset as not 'proper mission'. This misses the heart of what is a spirit led dynamic. Their whole life journey, at its best, flowed out of relationship with Jesus and from their contemplation and worship of the Trinity. It wasn't part of a twenty-first century 'to do' list. It was the intentional and at times the unintentional overflow of the wonder of relationship with Him. So whether in the cell, in the desert, by foot or by coracle there was an overflow in their journeying which impacted the world around them – how could it not?[37]

I've been ministered to recently by the words of a song by Jason Upton:

I don't know where I'm going;
I've been blinded by the truth.
Between the graveyard and the garden,
there's a road that leads to you.[38]

I love and am amused by the fact that one of Thomas Merton's famous prayers starts, 'My Lord God, I have no idea where I am going.' I think the reality of the life of faith is following the gentle leading of the Holy Spirit, and often the leading of our hearts. This is taking one step at a time. At times we don't know if we're on the right path, at times we may even feel like we're going in the opposite direction to where we feel we need to be, and almost always we don't know where this journey will take us... But there can be a deep joy in realising we are *free* to take this journey, and are loved so much that we are safe and secure, however we may feel.

Journeys can be in the spirit or in the physical. It may sound strange, but how about one time taking a journey somewhere for an hour, a day, or even a week, without knowing where you will end up, but seeing who and what the Lord brings your way as you journey? Or perhaps your journey to take is in the spirit. You could find a quiet place one time and offer the time

[37] Karen Lowe, *Wild Wandering* (Ceredigion: Shedhead Productions, 2006), p108.

[38] Jason Upton, 'Between the Graveyard and the Garden', from *On the Rim of the Visible World* (2010). © Jason Upton and Key of David Ministries, Inc. Used with permission. http://jasonupton.com/ (accessed 24th April 2014).

and any agenda you have to Him and let Him take you on an inner journey where only He knows the way. Our whole life is a journey towards our homeland. If we begin to realise this, we realise we don't have to be in control, but instead can let the Wild Goose set the tone for the adventure, and give us a Joy beyond all joys.

Learning from the Mystics: the centrality of love

If the Celtic Christians have shown us the value of journeying, then the Mystics show us that the journey is into love. At first glance, 'mystic' doesn't sound like a word you would associate with Christianity. However, if we consider that the term 'mystic' actually comes from the word 'mystery' then we start to get to the meaning. Mysticism applies to an area of our faith which is associated with experiencing the depths of 'who' God is, which obviously means that there are all sorts people and experiences that are spoken of as 'mystics' or 'Christian mysticism'. It does not deny, but is less focused upon the rational. Any experience that can be fully understood could hardly be described as 'mystery'. Also, Christian mysticism is not focused on experiences of the works of God (though it does not deny their place), but on experiencing the very nature of the Trinitarian God. For anyone with doubts about the term, let's make it clear that we are only referring to experiences of the God revealed in Scripture, and revealed through Jesus. Any other use of the term outside of this is not what we are discussing here.

There were about five characters from the fourteenth and fifteenth centuries who are referred to as the English Mystics, including Julian of Norwich, Margery Kempe, Richard Rolle and the unknown author of *The Cloud of Unknowing*. Also Teresa of Avila and John of the Cross from the sixteenth century are known as the Spanish Mystics, but the term does not stop at one group of people.

Often people referred to as Mystics have in one way or another given their lives to prayer, and in doing so have found that the God they seek is only to be found in association with 'love' – outside of love He can't be found, not even 0.000001% of Him! Those writers I have really connected with have inspired me in what they have found about God as they have gone deep with Him. They have testified to me that if I want to go deep into God then that is a journey into love. 'God is love', therefore love is at the centre of all that is most true about our existence. I'm going to have a quick look at two very different Mystics, the ones who have inspired me most, and how their experiences and teachings might help us in very different ways and seasons of our lives.

Julian of Norwich

For most of her life, Julian lived as an anchoress, which is another word for a hermit or a solitary. In her day in England, those with a calling to live alone in prayer would often live just outside a city or town, on the edge... Others lived alone within their communities, as she did, in a cell attached to a church building where people would come and speak to her through a hatch for spiritual advice, but except for this she was alone in prayer.

Julian had a series of 16 visions when she was in her early thirties, and it seems as if a lot of her life was spent seeking to 'understand' what she had received. What she saw were aspects of the sufferings of Jesus, and as she gave a lifetime to reflecting on these she came to conclude:

> The love God most high has for our soul is so great that it surpasses understanding. No created being can comprehend how much, and how sweetly, and how tenderly our maker loves us.[39]

After considering the reality of human sin and suffering in the face of these revelations, the words that were spoken to her,

---

[39] Llewellyn, *Enfolded in Love*, p15.

'But all shall be well, and all shall be well, and all manner of thing shall be well,'[40] seemed to sum up all that Julian had seen. She said that those words were spoken to her, 'so kindly and without a hint of blame.'[41]

One of her simpler revelations, I think, gives us a glimpse into Julian's character:

> He showed me a little thing, the size of a hazelnut, in the palm of my hand, and I thought, 'What can this be?' And an answer came, 'It is all that is made'. I marvelled that it could last, for I thought it might have crumbled to nothing, it was so small. And the answer came into my mind, 'It lasts and ever shall because God loves it'. And all things have their being through the love of God. In this little thing I saw three truths. The first is that God made it. The second is that God loves it. The third is that God looks after it.[42]

Julian's experiences were multicoloured and visionary, involving all her senses. She saw, she heard, she felt, she sensed, she encountered. God came to her as she was thought to be dying with an illness, He revealed His love to her as a love that could be touched, encountered and felt, and she recovered and lived another 50 years or so to reflect on these experiences.

Sometimes we just need Him to come and hold us and encounter us with love in a way we can reach out to, touch and feel and know. He loves to do this... If this is what you're experiencing, enjoy it. Let Him love on you like never before.

---

[40] Llewellyn, *Enfolded in Love*, p23.
[41] Llewellyn, *Enfolded in Love*, p23.
[42] Llewellyn, *Enfolded in Love*, p11.

John of the Cross

St John of the Cross was a Spanish Carmelite friar and friends with Teresa of Avila, who was 25 years older than him. Together they sought to reform the Carmelite order they were part of. He was imprisoned for nine months in 1577 by friars opposed to his reforms. John found that not only did the prison have its own deprivations, but at the very hour he needed God most, in those long months in prison, it 'seemed' as though His presence abandoned him. However, in time, he came to see that, though it had seemed like that, God's apparent absence was in fact Him revealing His love in an even deeper way. He gradually awakened to a deeper sense of the love of God which aided all his spiritual writings. John wrote about an experience of the love of God that is deeper than can be experienced by the mind, will and emotions, but is known purely in the heart:

> How gently and lovingly you wake in my heart, where in secret you dwell alone; and in your sweet breathing, filled with good and glory, how tenderly you swell my heart with love.[43]

This can really help us in times where we don't feel like God acts in the way we would like, or where we feel abandoned by Him... The truth is He never abandons us; He is always working in love. Yes, sometimes there are other reasons as to why it is hard to feel His presence, but sometimes He is leading us from living out of our souls to living out of our spirits. God is spirit, and the love of God is received most deeply in spirit. He never causes the sufferings we experience... but He is always with us and He never abandons us in our sufferings. He is *always* there.

---

[43] *The Collected Works of St John of the Cross* quoted in *The Story of Christian Spirituality* (Oxford: Lion, 2001), p211.

John also taught that there can come a time on the spiritual journey where the soul is no longer able to connect with God through the imagination, understanding or natural faculties it possesses. It begins to lose all desire for meditation on Scripture and other ways it has encountered God in the past. His teaching is that once this is discerned to be God, it is most valuable for the person to stop all he/she is doing, rather than fight against the Holy Spirit, and let Him work in this deep silence He is bringing.

This is one of my favourite quotes of John's:

> Say not, therefore: 'Oh the soul is making no progress, for it is doing nothing!' For if it is true that it is doing nothing, then by this very fact that it is doing nothing, I will now prove to you that it is doing a great deal.[44]

There we have it – there is a type of 'doing nothing' that is of the Holy Spirit! I know this is a very unpopular idea in our world, but it's true.

The point is that ultimately God's love is not dependent on us; it is not even dependent on us being able to 'experience' it. When we stop being able to 'experience' it, His love goes deeper. When we can't feel His embrace, we are still being embraced – we can stop and gaze in contemplation at this love that is deeper than any word, picture or thought. Along the journey into love, we can let go of all our efforts to make love be there, and simply begin to realise love is there, always there!

---

[44] St John of the Cross, *Living Flame of Love* (London: Burns and Oates, 1977), p186.

Our lives

Just a short look at these two Mystics shows us a glimpse of love in all its varied forms. Julian's encounters, for me, make me think of times on my journey where God's love has been so clear to all my senses, emotions and imaginative abilities. John's connect with times when the love of God is hidden in the depth at which it works. Both are part of the same picture, the same God, the same loving Father. What they have in common is that they show us that any experience of Him is to be found in association with love.

As one anonymous Carthusian writer put it:

> Never forget that God is love, and that the definition of any being indicates the limits of that being. Thus the 'limits' of God are infinite love: He is bound to love. His 'whole' is in love and love's 'whole' is in Him. We have no right therefore, to see anything but love in Him. Indeed, *there is no fear in love; but perfect love casteth out fear*. Dismiss altogether, then, from your thoughts this distressing fear, which died on the cross – nay, even in the Crib. Keep up your heart and rejoice in Him Who 'is', and is Love.[45]

May you see the centrality of love and may you never lose heart on your journey into love. As you walk the road of love, you may well find, as Jason Upton recently wrote in a song, that 'Love is a winding road',[46] but be sure that wherever you are on the road, 'love' is always, always, always, no matter what, surrounding that part of your travels!

---

[45] A Carthusian, *They Speak by Silences* (Herefordshire: Gracewing Publishing, 2006), p51.

[46] Jason Upton, 'Love is a winding road', from *Glimpse* (2012). © copyright: Jason Upton and Key of David, Inc. Used with permission.

Mystery: loved in your uniqueness

Did you know that you are a mystery?

You may feel amused at that question, but I mean it... the depths of who you are, are too mysterious to be put into words. Equally the depths of who God is are mystery... too great to be put into words.

For me, mystery is about uniqueness. There is a place inside your heart where you are most yourself. It is in this place, where you are most uniquely you in a way that no other person can be, that you are able to encounter the love of God.

> It is precisely where we are most alone, most unique, most ourselves, that God is closest to us. That is where we experience God as the divine, loving Father, who knows us better than we know ourselves.[47]

Often our deepest wounds come from not really being loved or seen in the place where we are most ourselves... Often we have not been truly understood as the people that we are – and this wounding is difficult to handle. For instance, you may be a gentle character, but those around you may have been louder and not able to understand your gentleness.

There are many ways this wounding can happen...

There are so many parts to our hearts...

But the deeper you go into the heart of God, or into your own heart, the more you find a silence and a quietness that may at times feel like nothing... But, in fact, the truth is that these depths are so beyond our experience that it is not possible on

---

[47] Henri J. M. Nouwen, *The Only Necessary Thing*, compiled and edited by Wendy Wilson Greer (London: Darton, Longman and Todd, Ltd, 2000), pp43-44.

earth to experience the depths of yourself, let alone the depths of God – we are a mystery even to ourselves!

This enables us to stop trying to understand everything as if one day we will get to what it really means to live. The depths of our uniqueness are known only to God, and there in that still place, we are loved a lot!

Bibliography

Burpo, Todd with Lynn Vincent, *Heaven is for Real*, Nashville: Thomas Nelson (2010)

Jordan, James, *Sonship*, Taupo, New Zealand: Tree of life Media (2012)

Johnson, Bill, *When Heaven Invades Earth*, Shippensburg: Treasure House, an imprint of Destiny Image Publishers, Inc (2003)

Julian of Norwich, *Revelations of Divine Love*, London: Penguin Books Ltd (1998)

Julian of Norwich, *In Love Enclosed*, London: Darton, Longman and Todd Ltd (2004)

Julian of Norwich, *Enfolded in Love*, London: Darton, Longman and Todd Ltd (2009)

Lowe, Karen, *Wild Wandering*, Ceredigion: Shedhead Productions (2006)

McCaffrey, James, *The Fire of Love: Praying with Therese of Lisieux*, Norfolk: Canterbury Press (1998)

Merton, Thomas, *New Seeds of Contemplation*, London: Burns and Oates, a Continuum imprint (2002)

Mursell, Gordon (ed.), *The Story of Christian Spirituality*, Oxford: Lion Publishing (2001)

Nygaard, Solveig, *Seasons of the Soul*, Copyright: Liquid Productions (2012)

Nouwen, Henri, *The Way of the Heart: The Spirituality of the Desert Fathers and Mothers*, New York: Harper One an imprint of Harper Collins Publishers (1991)

Nouwen, Henri, *The Only Necessary Thing*, compiled and edited by Wendy Wilson Greer, London: Darton, Longman and Todd, Ltd (2000)

Nouwen, Henri, in conversation with Philip Roderick, *Beloved*, Norfolk: Canterbury Press, (2007)

Sheets, Dutch, *Intercessory Prayer*, California, USA: Regal (1996)

St John of the Cross, *Living Flame of Love*, London: Burns and Oates (1977)

Winter, Jack, *The Homecoming*, Seattle: YWAM Publishing (1997)

A Carthusian, *They Speak by Silences*, Herefordshire: Gracewing Publishing (2006)

Unknown Author, *The Cloud of Unknowing*, edited by Evelyn Underhill, Mineola, NY: Dover Publications Inc (2003)

Urban Retreat

The Urban Retreat is a space for personal time with God. Created to be an easily accessible oasis, aside from the demands of daily life, it is a place for individuals to come and find rest, rebalancing and refreshing. We encourage peace and perspective which restore the soul and strengthen the spirit, through intimacy with the Father, Son and Holy Spirit. It is a prayer centre, designed to encourage the many forms that prayer can take. The emphasis is on alone time with God, believing that just as our Lord Jesus took time away from others to be with His Father, we are invited to follow in His example and find opportunities to do the same.

In the Retreat you will find spaces to soak in His loving presence, to intercede for Watford, to worship Him through creativity, music, prayer and natural beauty, and to spend time in complete solitude with the Lord. We invite you to learn from others, both ancient and modern, who have discovered ways of exploring the mysteries and wonders of God, with books, materials and suggestions to help you connect with Him.

We believe that better is one day in His courts than a thousand elsewhere. We invite you to come to the Retreat, to enter into His courts, to seek and to find, to rest and to be restored.

The Urban Retreat is membership-based, open to members Monday to Friday, 9.30am – 5.30pm and Saturdays, 11.30am – 3.30pm. Membership is available to those with a significant connection with Watford who desire to come and meet with our Lord Jesus Christ.